Other Books by
John Gregory Dunne

Delano
The Studio

VEGAS

A
MEMOIR
OF
A
DARK
SEASON

JOHN GREGORY DUNNE

VEGAS

A

MEMOIR

OF

A

DARK

SEASON

RANDOM HOUSE NEW YORK

917.93
D

Library of Congress Cataloging in Publication Data
Dunne, John Gregory, 1932–
Vegas: a memoir of a dark season.
Autobiographical.
1. Dunne, John Gregory, 1932–   I. Title
CT275.D88227A3   917.93' 13' 030924 [B]   73–5034
ISBN 0–394–46165–7

Manufactured in the United States of America

2 4 6 8 9 7 5 3

First Edition

For
Noel E. Parmentel, Jr.

Ite missa est.
Deo gratias.

This is a fiction which recalls a time both real and imagined. There are, for example, comics, prostitutes and private detectives in Las Vegas; there is no Jackie Kasey, no Artha Ging, no Buster Mano. I am more or less "I," he and she less than more he and she.

*Like everything which is not the
result of fleeting emotion but of time
and will, any marriage, happy or unhappy,
is infinitely more interesting and
significant than any romance, however
passionate.*

—W.H. Auden

Nobody I know goes to Las Vegas.

—Margot Hentoff

LAS VEGAS, CLARK
COUNTY, NEVADA (Lat: 36° 11′ N; Long: 115°
08′ W); first settled by a band of Mormons in 1855
on instructions from Brigham Young; abandoned
by the Mormons following a series of Paiute Indian
raids. The United States cavalry established an outpost on the site of Las Vegas during the Civil War
to protect the travel route to Southern California.
The city was officially founded on May 15, 1905,
but did not begin to flourish until 1931, when the
state of Nevada legalized gambling. Today the center of a metropolis of nearly 300,000 people. It has
143 churches, 159 Boy Scout troops, 93 public and
parochial schools, all of which ban the teaching of
sex education, 220 registered housing subdivisions,
Nellis Air Force Base, "largest Air Force installation
in the free world," 25,596 hotel and motel rooms,
1,000 gaming tables and 16,000 slot machines. Las
Vegas means "The Meadows," and has a suicide
rate twice the national average.

PART

1

ONE

In the summer of my nervous breakdown, I went to live in Las Vegas, Clark County, Nevada. It had been a bad spring, it had been a bad winter, it had been a bad year. In the fall I had gone to take an insurance physical. The insurance office was on the nineteenth floor of an antiseptic new building on Wilshire Boulevard in Los Angeles. It was surrounded on every side by a moat-like parking lot, every parking space neatly marked by diagonal lines, white for transient parking, yellow for monthly parking, green for the building's maintenance personnel. From the window in the doctor's office I could look across the street at a neo-Polynesian barn, headquarters of one of the largest rental agencies in Los Angeles. Revolving on the roof of the building was a neon sign advertising

EVERYTHING FOR THE PARTY OR THE SICK ROOM

Banquet Tables   *Wheelchairs*
Card Tables   *Walkers*

China	*Traction Lifters*
Silver	*Commodes*
Glasses	*Oxygen*
Bars	*IPPB Units*
Tents	*Crutches*
Canopies	*Whirlpools*

The examining physician's name was Virgil Isador Kerides. He was, he informed me, a Greek Jew. He said it was a problem. I am always being told things like that on first meeting, being told by strange women that they have cancer of the uterus, by men on airplanes that they have a colored mistress in St. Louis. Never black, never Negro, always "colored." I have never learned how to react, never comprehended why I am selected for these intimacies. Perhaps it is a penance for the deaf ear I turn to the problems of friends. I cannot bear to listen to why they are leaving their wives or how they are treating their alcoholism. "Really," I say to these strangers with uterine malignancies, or "I see." I never do see.

What I did see about Virgil Isador Kerides was that he was wearing one black shoe and one brown shoe and that a daub of egg yolk had adhered to his tie. I am interested in things like that, as I am interested in the layout and color coding of parking lots. I am interested in overheard conversations in restaurants, in the mosaic of petty treasons that decorate small lives. It is a hobby without emotional investment. I wonder by what act of fate a promising medical student becomes an aging doctor for an insurance company, wearing one black and one brown shoe, a Vaseline-coated plastic glove on his hand, every day invading and investigating the rectums of strangers. I wonder and do not ask. My wife says I am clinically detached.

Virgil Isador Kerides stripped the plastic glove from his hand and began taking my blood pressure. He had noted on my form that I was a writer. He said that he was interested in writing. He thought he would try his hand at it. There were a number of medical shows on television that season. He wondered if they would need a technical adviser. I suggested he write the producers.

"I'm probably too late," he said. "I've always been too late."

"Really," I said.

"Maybe I could write an exposé of the medical shows for *TV Guide.*"

"Maybe."

He busied himself with my chart. Blood pressure normal. EKG normal. EEG normal. Prostate normal. No known diseases. Chronic indigestion probably due to overweight. The policy was for $100,000, payments $450 per quarter. I was thirty-seven years old and I was insurable, a good risk.

I put on my clothes. There was one thing, Virgil Isador Kerides said. It was not medical, it would not hold up the issuing of the policy. Had anyone ever told me that I had soft shoulders?

I asked what it meant.

"Nothing. They're just . . . soft. You've got soft shoulders."

Soft shoulders. If ever there seemed a perfect metaphor for my life that season, that was it. I did not seek another diagnosis. I was not concerned about muscular atrophy or neurological disintegration or pulpy bone marrow. With some dim psychic instinct Virgil Isador Kerides, who found it a problem being a Greek Jew, had intuited what I already knew, that there were other renegade cells eating away at the tissues of my life.

The metastasis had started a year or two before. When I was younger, and other people turned thirty-five, I had found it amusing to send a two-word birthday telegram. The wire simply read, "Halfway home." But the spring I reached thirty-five, the joke suddenly seemed pallid. Perhaps it was because I began to find the names of classmates appearing in the obituary notes of my college alumni magazine. "After a short illness . . ." the notice would begin. It was a chilling phrase. There was at least something youthful and abandoned about a drunken-driving accident or skiing into a tree. I began to note in my diary the date of my annual medical checkup. I examined myself for lumps and bumps. I heard with dark dread a doctor tell me that he was sending a piece of tissue "down for a biopsy." I became quite simply, for no real reason, terrified of dying.

The obsession evidenced itself in small ways at first. I hated to fly on planes with minor celebrities and second-string newscasters and the failed offspring of prominent people. I got off a crowded flight once rather than sit next to Elliott Roosevelt. The headline had already formed in my mind: "Crash Kills FDR Son and 92 Others." There were reminders of mortality everywhere. Snowbound in a motel in Montana, I opened a letter that had been forwarded to me. I did not know

who sent it, there was no return address. All it con-
tained was a one-inch clip from *The New York Times:*
someone I had known at school had fallen in front of
the 8:12 commuter train from Noroton to Grand Central and was killed instantly. I had not even particularly
liked this fellow, but there in that Best Western Motel
in Great Falls, Montana, I remembered with febrile
clarity the last time I had seen him. It was perhaps
fifteen years earlier, the night before he went into the
Marine Corps. I had run into him on the street in New
York, and as a going-away present I bought him what
in the fifties used to be called "a piece of ass." The girl
was a prostitute who lived in an orange-painted basement apartment over near the East River. She charged
twenty dollars for what she referred to as "two pops."
The girl did not understand that I did not want to share
in the present, nor did I even want to watch. Instead I
sat in her living room leafing through a portfolio of
dirty pictures. I could hear them bargaining in the next
room over a third pop. He did not wish to pay, she tried
to persuade him to get me to ante up another ten dollars. It was nearly dawn when we left the apartment.
His train for Quantico pulled out of Penn Station at
6:30 A.M. We walked through the deserted streets and
we had nothing to say. We shook hands at the gate; the
next time I heard of him was after his appointment with
the 8:12 out of Noroton.

I began to wonder if my death would merit a
"Milestone" in *Time.* Would the editors consider me
Milestone material? ("He used to work here," I could
imagine them saying, "never made senior editor."

"What did he do after he left. Or was he fired?"

"Left, I think."

"Wrote a couple of books."

"Really."

"It's between him and that Dionne who checked out."

"Let's go for the quint.")

My temper, always volatile, turned explosive. One day on Sunset Boulevard a boy in an Austin-Healey sideswiped me and drove my car up onto the sidewalk. "You motherfucker," I screamed after him.

The Austin-Healey ground to a halt. The boy and his girl friend got out of the car and walked back to mine. He was wearing a buckskin jacket and cowboy boots, she sandals, jeans and an Indian blouse with no bra. I surveyed her tits.

"What you call me?" the cowboy said.

"Motherfucker," I said. "M-O-T-H-E-R-F . . ."

"You want a belt in the mouth?"

"What are you trying to do? Impress the cunt? Mr. Tough?"

"Tougher than you, motherfucker."

We squared off there at high noon on Sunset Boulevard, across from where the Garden of Allah used to be, where Robert Benchley and Scott Fitzgerald and Dorothy Parker had lived, their conversation I am sure a good deal brighter than the "cunt" and "motherfucker" being bandied back and forth between the boy in buckskin and the thirty-seven-year-old lunatic in a gray Firebird convertible. I took the first swing, hitting him high on the cheekbone, and for my daring got a cowboy boot squarely between my testicles. I lay on the sidewalk, holding my nuts and moaning in pain, watching the boy and his girl drive insolently off in the Austin-Healey.

The empty days were riven with other indignities. I went to a doctor to see if there was any medical reason why I had been unable to conceive a child. Not that I even wanted to. My only child was adopted and there was no chance that anything produced by my genes could come close to equaling her. But it was something to do, a day-waster. The doctor said there were two ways to check my semen, either via what he called "self-gratification" or with the seed of coitus interruptus. I chose the former; since the semen had to be in his office no more than forty-five minutes after climax, there was a "Beat the Clock" ambience about the latter that I found intimidating. The timer raised his gun. Ready: On the mark: Get set: Go. Out of bed and into your clothes. The car engine was idling. East on Palos Verdes Drive. South on 26th Street in San Pedro. Onto the Harbor Freeway. Change over to the San Diego Freeway. Off at Wilshire Boulevard. If the lights were with you and the car was in tune, it was a forty-three-minute Emission Possible. Self-gratification seemed more meaningful.

The doctor's nurse gave me a natural lambskin rubber prophylactic and the directions to the men's room. I sat in a stall trying to coax some heft into my flaccid member, terrified that the cubicle door would be flung open and I discovered with a lubricated rubber dangling between my legs, like some refugee from a bus station or a Y.M.C.A. men's room. I tried to conjure up breasts and pudenda, a difficult task when the theme music was the constipated grunting from the adjoining stall. Someone at the urinal began crooning:

> *"You've got to live a little,*
> *Laugh a little,*
> *Always have the blues a little,*
> *That's the story of,*
> *That's the glory of*
> *Love, love, love."*

The minutes ticked away. I imagined the nurse in the doctor's office checking her watch, wondering what kind of auto-perversion I was into. I made a mental list of every woman I had ever had intercourse with. The number was twenty-eight and none of them were giving me any help. *Love, love, love.* Whom had I wanted to fuck and never had? Movie stars, the wives of friends, dogs, cows, anything. Nothing. *Love, love, love.* Carmella Manupelli, seventh grade, Verbum Dei School, Hartford, Connecticut, the first girl I ever knew who wore a brassiere, now a Little Sister of the Poor in Chicago. Bingo.

I put the rubber in a prescription box and gave it to the nurse. She accepted it as if it were a prune Danish from the coffee cart. I still had the condom's foil covering crumpled in my hand and did not know what to do with it. The reception-room wastebasket did not seem the place for it, so I just held it in my fist. I regarded the other patients, fairly certain that I had whacked off more recently, or at least more recently in a bizarre environment, than any of them.

It was nearly an hour before the results were in. The spermatozoa had passed the test.

"They won't win any races," the doctor said. "But they get there."

I asked the forgiveness of Mother Mary Stella

Mare, formerly Carmella Manupelli. The race was not always to the swift.

2

At home it was the familiar season of discontent. I sometimes had the feeling that we went from crisis to crisis like old repertory actors going from town to town, every crisis an opening night with new depths to plumb in the performance. I bought a jacknife; she said it was atavistic. I said that living with her was like living with one piranha fish. She said dealings with women aged people. One night we lay in bed without speaking. After a while she said, "Are you lying on my book?"

"Which book?"

"The one I was reading before. The cookbook."

I found it under the covers and handed it to her. It was Elizabeth David's *French Provincial Cooking* and was folded to a recipe for *tête de veau vinaigrette:* "When it is good, which is to say when it is served really tender and hot and you get a comparatively lean piece and the *vinaigrette* sauce has been well mixed, then it is quite good. More often, it is repellent."

In the morning, I said, "Did you finish the book?"

"It gave me a headache."

"Why?"

"The particular rhythm of the sentences. They upset my alpha waves."

In the absence of anything else, I began to drive, the freeways first, then longer expeditions, day-long excursions designed only to improve the quality of my consumption. I reconnoitered a clothing store in Santa Barbara, a Sears in San Diego. One morning I went out to buy a loaf of bread for breakfast and finally picked it up at a Safeway in San Francisco. It is 476 miles to San Francisco. On another foray, I was stopped outside San Luis Obispo for speeding and given a drunk test. I touched my nose and counted backward from one hundred and when the highway patrolman asked how many years of education I had completed, I replied, "Four years of Princeton." He looked at me queerly and let me go.

The driving expeditions became longer, more complicated. I went to Brawley for three days, to Ukiah for a week. Speed was the release, 135 m.p.h. flat-out, the risk of a blowout exhilarating. It was a time of carhops and cocktail waitresses. All day long I would stay in my motel room in El Centro or Lone Pine and watch "Dialing for Dollars" and "Secret Storm" and "The Newlywed Game." I lusted after Julia Child on "The French Chef." I would put a quarter into the Magic Fingers when she came on the air and lie on the bed and watch her prepare a quiche or a *coq au vin,* the mattress undulating while I concentrated with fertile imagination on all six feet two inches of the chef in her television kitchen. Nights I would cruise the coffee shops, and in the morning I would look in the mirror and see the beginnings of a dewlap around the neck.

One afternoon in the fall I said I was going to New York that night to watch the World Series. Not at the ball park, but on television. She never asked why our television set was not good enough; she understood.

She understood the driving and why I had not worked in over a year and the fear of dying and the necessity of taking the TWA red-eye to New York. I stayed at the apartment of a friend who was out of town. As it happened, his television set was out of order and I heard the World Series on the radio and in the evenings I would go to the Frank E. Campbell funeral home on Madison Avenue at 81st to see if I knew anyone who had died. I saw no one and never ventured out of the apartment except to go to Campbell's and to buy Oreo cookies and Heath bars at the delicatessen.

The World Series was over in five games. I needed to get in touch and still had not made a connection. I tried to sort out the primal experiences— birth, marriage, the first sexual encounter. I was twenty years old and she a prostitute of uncertain years. In the fifth inning of the last game of the Series, I checked the telephone book to see if she was still listed. She was still at the same address. I dialed the number. I wanted to see where the years had gone.

"Hello, Phyl, this is Philip." Philip was the name I had always used.

Her voice had the same huskiness. "Philip who, dear?"

"Philip from Princeton."

There was a long pause. "When was the last time I talked to you, dear?"

It had been nearly seventeen years, but I lied. "I guess about five years ago."

"Jesus, darling," she said, "I'm sixty-two years old."

3

In the spring I bought a baseball mitt for myself and one for my daughter. I was thirty-seven and she was three. I saw a Victor Mature Festival in a deserted closet-sized theater run by two homosexuals in Santa Monica, and followed it a few days later with a Lon McAllister Festival. The projectionist wore a fishnet tank shirt and laughed hysterically at *Home In Indiana.* I was the only person in the theater and he came down and talked to me until he had to change reels. He said he had a passion for Walter Brennan and that his father was an Air Force colonel and that he was moving to Cuzco the next day. Just cruising, he said, I'll just be cruising.

There was something about him that made me, for the first time in months, want to go back to work. There is a therapeutic aspect to reporting that few like to admit. What is a reporter except a kind of house detective, scavenging through the bureau drawers of men's lives, searching for the minor vice, the half-forgotten lapse that is stored away like a dirty pair of drawers. Reporting anesthetizes one's own problems. There is always someone in deeper emotional drift, or even grift, than you, someone to whom you can ladle out understanding as if it were a charitable contribution, one free meal from the psychic soup kitchen, just that one, no more, any more would entail responsibility, and responsibility is what one is trying to avoid in the first place.

The question was where to go to find that perfect place where one could look for salvation without commitment. And then one day I was driving on La Brea

Avenue in Hollywood and saw a new billboard high
atop the office of a credit dentist. On a brown field there
was a picture of an enormous roulette wheel and a
gold-lettered legend that said simply, with a Delphic
absence of apostrophe: VISIT LAS VEGAS BEFORE YOUR
NUMBERS UP.

  And so I did, barely.

TWO

"**M**ay I ask you a very personal question?"

The questioner was a trim man in his low forties, face evenly burnished with a reflector tan, blond hair neatly transformed by electrolysis into a distinguished widow's peak; his lime-colored alpaca cardigan was held together by two pearl buttons. It was four o'clock in the afternoon, I had just finished breakfast and I wondered just how personal any question could be that was asked next to the cash register at the coffee shop of the Mint Hotel in downtown Las Vegas. "Shoot," I said.

"How long have you been, you know, thin on top?"

My hand went involuntarily to the top of my head. I had been, as he said, "thin on top" since my mid-twenties. I never even thought much about it. My mother said it was because I did not wash my hair regularly; my father, she said, still had a full head of hair when he died. I did not remember ever actually washing my hair, but then I could not have gone twenty years without a hair wash. "Ten, fifteen years," I said.

"Ever think of a piece?"

I looked at him blankly.

"A piece, a toupee," he said.

"No, not really." I had never seen a piece I had not been able to spot. Even now my eyes zeroed in on his electrolysis. It was not as good as John Wayne's net.

I shook my head and took my change from the cashier.

"What day is it?" he said.

"Thursday."

"I can put you into a piece by Monday morning," he said. "Not even your mother could tell." He touched the hair curling over my ears. "A little bland," he said. "But easy to match. Henna highlights, if you want. Three different lengths. Freshly cut, well-groomed and modishly long."

"No, thanks."

"Here's my card. Call me."

The card said, WAYNE FREY, PIECE WORK.

"You'd be surprised the number of people in Vegas I've put into pieces," Wayne Frey said. "An entire pit crew at the Dunes." I pondered that. "People like to bet with well-groomed dealers. You ever stop to consider that?"

"I don't gamble."

He smiled triumphantly and tapped his finger against my chest. "Then you've got enough to buy a piece."

"I'll pass."

"Call me. What's your handle?"

I told him.

"I'll be hearing from you, John," Wayne Frey

said. He swept out into the casino and sat down at a blackjack table. The dealer was as bald as an egg. I tried to imagine myself in a piece. I had heard once that bald men have more sexual virility. Thank God for something.

It was my second day in Las Vegas and I was staying at the Mint until I was able to find an apartment. An old bellhop had brought me to my room, a corrupted Grant Wood American Gothic type with rimless glasses and a light snow of dandruff on the shoulders of his bright red bellman's uniform. He was so feeble that he was hardly able to hassle my bags. He checked the water spigots and the lights, opened the dresser drawer, lyricized about the size of the closets and the number of hangers therein, an old man with small seeds of rheum in the corners of his eyes and no color in his hair, and when I gave him a two-dollar tip, he cleared the mucous rattle from his throat and said, "If you gamble, sir, good luck, and if you need a little company, you just give me a ring, hear?"

I was so astounded that I could not even ask for particulars. It was like discovering that an old uncle, the failed one whose taco franchise had gone bankrupt, had started pimping.

"As I was saying, you just get in touch with me or Nate, that's the other bellman, he's the colored, but he's a nice boy, Nate." He cleared his throat again and I watched his Adam's apple bob as he swallowed the hawker. His accent was Western, a nasal whine combined with an odd obsequiousness. The idea of a sexual conspiracy between me and this old man filled me with dread. "Nice and clean, the girls, young and good-looking."

I tried to herd him toward the door.

"You need any more hangers, too, you just call me. Ask for Dan. We got nothing but wooden hangers here. Not like some places, which give you the wire jobs. A gentleman like you can't hang his coat proper from a wire job."

I opened the door.

"Clean," he whispered from the corridor. "Young and good-looking."

2

I drove. A little red rented Pinto. Full factory air, tinted windshield, radio, heater, white sidewalls, seven dollars a day, seven cents a mile, best rental-car bargain in Clark County. I drove down the Strip. County land, not part of the city of Vegas; the heat on the Strip was sheriff's department heat, not the LVPD. Very heavy heat, don't mess with it, yes, Officer, no, Officer heat. The Strip was not much to look at by day. Flat and two-dimensional. An idiot Disneyland of architectural parabolas, overloaded utility poles, celestial hamburger stands and gimcrackery fairy palaces. Wait until you see it at night, I was told. When the lights are on. I waited. At night it was an idiot Disneyland with lights.

"I knew Ben."

"No shit."

"In '47."

"The Flamingo?"

"A very warm personal friend."

In my first three days in Vegas, I met eleven

people who said they were very warm personal friends
of the late Benjamin Siegel, who detested the nickname
"Bugsy." They said it as if they were saying they knew
Cecil Rhodes or Henry Stanley. A man ahead of his
time. The first imperialist of the Strip. The man who
made this town what it is today. Ben. Never Bugsy.
"Ben always packed iron." "I hear twelve notches on
Ben's iron." "That's on the light side, I hear."
    "No shit?"
    "No shit."
    "Ahead of his time, Ben."
    The Fabulous Flamingo was Ben's monument.
Check that: his pyramid. Opened in 1946. Changed the
face of the Strip. Ahead of his time, Ben. His very warm
personal friends were younger then. No varicose veins
in 1946. A lot more hair. Steam in the old cockeroo four
or five times a night. Every night. Couldn't keep it bent.
Poor Ben. The books wouldn't tally. Accounting diffi-
culties. Could happen to anyone. Except it happened to
Ben. And something else happened to Ben. On June 20,
1947. At 808 North Linden Drive, Beverly Hills, California. Bang, bang. Through Virginia Hill's window.
The late Ben Siegel. A man ahead of his time.
    "I was in Miami that night," the first man with
varicose veins said.
    "I was in Chi," the second man with varicose
veins said.

    I drove some more. Through Artesian Heights
and Sierra Vista Ranchos and Equestrian Estates and
Camelot Gardens. Subdivision followed on subdivision.
Vegas was less than 50,000 when Ben cooled. Today—
nearly 300,000. Tomorrow—"Seven figures." That was
the way the man in the county supervisor's office said

it: not a million, but "seven figures." I liked the sound
of it. And drove some more. Out past Nellis AFB.
Home of the 474th TFW—F-111 Roadrunners. A lot
of plane. A lot of mobile-home sites out by Nellis. And
a lot more promised by Amfac. Back into town.
Through the West Side. The West Side was the black
part of Vegas. A bungalow slum. Forty thousand blacks
in Vegas. A couple of dozen dealing blackjack on the
Strip. The rest were maids or, as I was told, in "maintenance."

I drove some more. West on Sahara Boulevard,
past the Strip, past the Be-Jak ranch, until the road just
petered out in the desert. A couple of rattlesnakes
sunned themselves by a sign that said: "Pavement Ends.
Road Closed. Travel At Own Risk." The sign was
pockmarked with bullet holes; the time and the temperature were still plainly visible in the Sahara Tower. The
side of the road out there on West Sahara Boulevard
resembled the trail of an army in full retreat. Carcasses
of cars, refrigerators, propane heaters, furniture with
the stuffing ripped out, a dump that was not even an
official dump. Just a place in the desert to dump the
leavings of a lifetime, out past the Be-Jak ranch before
the pavement ended. Tires, old radios, television sets
with no picture tubes, stoves, washing machines, bicy-
cles, ironing boards, supermarket carts, air-conditioning units. Why here? Why did so many people travel
out here past the Be-Jak ranch to junk their belongings?
I could not find an answer, but today, years later, that
stretch of highway out on the edge of the desert seems
a more vivid image of Vegas than the lights of the Strip
that even then were struggling against the summer twilight.

3

I stayed at the Mint until I was able to find an apartment. I looked at twenty-three in all, each more depressing than the last, the units like stalags on either side of the Strip. There were flats with "blue decor" and others with "green decor"; everything was color complemented. In each there was a four-piece "suite" in the living room: settee, two chairs and a coffee table, and a single small painting, usually of a harbor, a detail of gold sails on a color-keyed blue or green seascape.

I met Dora at a little place off Karen Avenue, behind the Sahara Hotel. The entry to the courtyard was all glass brick and there was a metal gate topped with fleur-de-lis spikes. I could see Dora through the gate, clumping around the swimming pool in the middle of the courtyard, carrying a pail and a dry mop. She was about fifty, with pale blond hair thinned by too much peroxide piled atop her head, pinched features and a long nose humped in the middle. She looked like one of those women who had spent too many hours in front of a slot machine. She was wearing a muumuu and support hose and although she saw me she ignored my first three rings.

"She's not here," Dora said finally. "Threw her out yesterday." I did not have a clue who "she" was. "Yes, sir, threw the bitch out." Dora's voice rose, as if she were issuing a warning to any other tenants hiding behind the drawn curtains and the tinfoil crimped in the windows to ward off the heat. "Told her I'd tell Ralph Lamb about her."

"Who's Ralph Lamb?"

"Sheriff, Clark County, Nevada, that's who," Dora said. "Won't have her type around here. I check."

I had an idea what type she meant, but did not ask. "I'm just looking for a place."

"Could have had hers you got here sooner," Dora said. "Just rented it to a pit boss at the Dunes. Real nice fella. Wife just left him." She was now at the gate. She had orthopedic shoes and a slight limp.

"You know any other places?"

"Not as nice as this."

"The next nicest."

"I'll make you some tea. I go for Salada on an afternoon like this. Cools you off."

She opened the gate and I followed her around the pool to a ground-floor apartment on the other side of the courtyard. She limped into her kitchen. "Real nice place I run here. Just pit bosses and professional people. Never let a girl live alone though."

"Why not?"

"Always end up having to call Ralph Lamb about them." She came from the kitchen with a tray and two glasses of iced tea. "That Ralph Lamb will run them out of town soon enough if he wants my vote."

Dora settled into a rocking chair by an electric fire that gave out no heat, only a faked glow over painted burning logs. "Hot," she said.

"Hot."

She hitched up her muumuu. "Don't mind if I get comfortable, do you?"

I shook my head. I tried not to gulp the Salada. I tried to fix my attention on some undissolved flecks of instant tea in my glass. She pulled the support hose off her left leg. Underneath the thick beige stocking was an artificial limb. She unhooked the brace and stood the leg against the electric fire.

"Whooosh, it's hot," Dora said.

What remained of her leg looked like an immense white sausage. "Must be a hundred," I said desperately.

"A hundred and six," she said. "You feel better now?"

I nodded. I was searching for an exit line.

She kneaded the globules of flesh on her stump. "Used to turn Harry Hyams on when I did this," she said suddenly, as if it were the most natural thing in the world to say. "My ex. Unbuckle that peg leg and he'd just start getting hot." She smiled lasciviously. "Want some more tea?"

"No, thanks."

"Got to get it yourself, I'm afraid," she said, pointing to her cork leg. It was as if she had not heard. She rocked contentedly, watching the electric flames over the painted logs as if they were real. "Really made him hot."

"Who?"

"Harry Hyams," she said. "Do anything for you?"

I did not know what to say. I could not take my eyes off the white hatchwork scar tissue where the stitches had been.

"It takes all kinds, I guess," Dora said. "It was a malignant hematoma that did it." She was lost in reverie. "Really turned him on."

I wanted to know more about Harry Hyams, who he was, where he had gone, but not enough to follow in his footsteps. Dora was still rocking as I walked out into the sunlit courtyard, around the swimming pool to the gate. I knew she was still watching me through her open door. As the gate closed behind me, I heard her croon, "It really made Harry Hyams hot."

I finally found a place on Desert Inn Road. It was called the Royal Polynesian, and in each unit there was a black-and-white television set, a hot plate, a plastic dinner service for two and two peanut-butter jars reincarnated as water glasses. The center of social activity at the Royal Polynesian was the swimming pool. Every afternoon it was full of aging show girls, their looks and figures still fairly intact, women without men, careful not to let their hair get wet in the pool.

It seemed the perfect place to spend that summer, a paradigm of anti-life. I did not gamble, cared not at all about the Mob and even less about Howard Hughes. But there were other stories and other people, and there were days when I told myself that through the travail of others I might come to grips with myself, that I might, as it were, find absolution through voyeurism. Those were the good days.

PART

2

THREE

In her five years in Vegas, Artha had kept the following statistics. She had turned 1,203 tricks with 1,076 different johns. Ninety-seven tricks had been unable to get an erection, 214 came before penetration. She had engaged in anal intercourse eighty-eight times and fellatio 863 times. She had had thirteen professional lesbian contacts and three non-professional, and had been hired for "multiples," or group sex, fifty-four times. She had been whipped professionally eleven times and in turn had strapped tricks with a belt twenty-three times and with a horse-whip once. The masochists generally had preferred to get whipped around the genitals, the sadists to whip her buttocks. One client had paid her three hundred dollars to clip off her pubic hair, which he then put in a Mason jar; she never saw him again. She had been defecated on six times, urinated on thirteen times; she on her part had defecated on twelve tricks and urinated on twenty-two. Her vagina had been successfully penetrated by penises, dildos, bottles, bananas, frankfurters, candles and vibrators, and unsuccessfully by a pop-top can of Fresca.

She had taken accounting in high school in Milwaukee and kept the statistics in a loose-leaf three-ring binder notebook. There was a check mark for each occurrence, and a date, and at the bottom of a column the ledger was totted up. She said that she kept her records in lieu of keeping a diary, making each entry in green ink with an old Parker 51 fountain pen. The statistics were neatly marked on accounting paper that she bought in a stationery store in the Maryland Parkway shopping mall, and the notebook separated by file dividers with such headings as "Sucking" and "Whipping"; she did not know the meaning of either "fellatio" or "cunnilingus," and when I defined them for her she thought the words were "cute."

Artha was running behind schedule. From the bedroom window in her apartment near the Ice Palace, she could see the temperature-clock in the tower of the Sahara Hotel, first the time—8:17—then the temperature reading—already 88°. The air conditioner in her apartment bedroom was not working. Four nights before, a sixty-three-year old appliance salesman from Kansas City, in Vegas for the Kelvinator convention, had thrown her portable hair dryer at it after ejaculating prematurely in Artha's bathroom as she was washing his penis with soap and warm water. The hair dryer was bent and broken beyond repair. Artha had tried to return it to the Montgomery Ward outlet in the Sunrise Shopping Center where it had been purchased, but the buyer in the notions department said that the manufacturer would not honor the warranty, as the damage seemed clearly the result of owner neglect. Artha had called the buyer a dyke, and when the buyer then summoned a store policeman, Artha had called him a spade cocksucker. Despite these entreaties, Montgomery Ward still refused to replace the hair dryer. And then the appliance salesman, who had stayed with Artha for two days, disappeared while taking his dirty underwear to a laundromat in Vegas Village. He had left his suitcase in Artha's apartment, and when he did not return she had thrown it out, first checking the contents and finding nothing but some clean shirts, two old copies of *Cavalier* magazine and the Kelvinator convention brochure and schedule of events.

8:22 on the Sahara clock. The air-conditioning repairman was due at noon. Artha would have to cut her 11:30 class at the Manhattan Beauty College in order to let him into the apartment. She kept her school clothes in a closet separate from her casual and her working clothes. She chose a long-sleeved cotton paisley dress and flat beige sandals. No boots at school. Nor did she ever wear a brassiere to the Manhattan Beauty College. She only wore a bra in the evening to enhance her décolletage. The course at the Manhattan Beauty College cost $1,365 and lasted for 1,800 hours spread out over forty-seven weeks. Artha had decided to take the cosmetology course so that she might have something to fall back on when she retired from prostitution. She still intended to moonlight as a prostitute when she finished the course. She liked to say that she would set a wife's hair by day and suck her husband's cock by night. She thought it was a cute joke.

Artha selected a straight fall from her wig closet. There were twenty-one different wigs and falls in the closet, all brunette. She liked to say that she was a natural brunette, although one St. Patrick's Day when she was nineteen and working in a two-girl house in a lumber camp in Antigo, Wisconsin, she had dyed her pubic hair green. 8:26. Time for one poem. Three years before, a coffee-shop hostess at the Frontier Hotel on the Strip had given her a copy of Sara Teasdale's collected poems. The coffee-shop hostess had been in love with her, and now every morning Artha read at least one poem before leaving the apartment. She likened it to people who read the Bible every day. She said it made her feel peaceful. In spare moments, Artha wrote poetry herself, often in the Teasdale manner. Sometimes, while in a casino waiting for a late date, she would scribble a poem on the back of a keno card.

> *Star light,*
> *Moon bright,*
> *Will I save my life tonight?*
> *In the stillness of the morn*
> *The question is,*
> *Why was I born?*

8:32. The coffee-shop hostess had turned over in a Pontiac GTO between Baker and Barstow at a speed estimated by the California Highway Patrol at 110 miles per hour. She had been thrown from the car and her neck snapped like a wishbone, but beyond that she had been relatively unmarked, except that her left thumb had been severed from the rest of her hand. The thumb was never found in the desert alkali dust. It was the missing thumb that bothered Artha even more than her friend's death. She thought the Highway Patrol should have spent more time looking in the desert for the lost digit. It seemed wrong to her for someone not to be buried whole.

8:40. Artha picked up her bag and textbook and walked to her Dodge Dart in the apartment parking lot. She had only three more payments to make on the Dart, and then she planned to turn it in for an AMC Gremlin. Once she had test-driven a Fiat, but her opinion was that driving a Fiat was like fucking an Italian, or "ginney," as Artha called all Italians— it promised more than it gave. The temperature in the Sahara Tower now read 90°. The ride downtown to the Manhattan Beauty College took fifteen minutes from her apartment. Artha knew that she would be late for school, but the test that morning would not begin before nine. The instructor, Mr. Luigi, always made allowances for latecomers. The test was in the theory of facial massage.

2

Artha did not know Buster Mano, but Buster Mano knew Artha. Buster was a large comfortable man in his late forties, well read for a private detective, especially in the works of Martin Luther. Buster had become interested in Luther after learning that the Wittenberg monk was constipated. Constipation was a subject never far from Buster Mano's mind. He claimed he had a blocked colon, but never had it corrected because, as he said, he was "afraid of the knife." Once he was sure of someone, Buster abandoned all side about his constipation and farted openly and frequently, hitching up his buttocks for maximum comfort and efficacy.

"Popcorn farts," he would call them, "all noise, no stink."

Buster had spent twenty-two years in a medium-sized police department in a medium-sized city in the Midwest, where he had a tract house, a mortgage, and two cars, both secondhand, both paid for. His wife got the menopause at thirty-two and his daughter got married at fifteen. What bewildered Buster about his daughter's marriage was that she was not even pregnant. He suspected that her marriage had something to do with the fact that his wife had taken her to a gynecologist to see if her hymen was still intact. She had met her husband a week later at an amusement park where he was passing out sample packages of Philip Morris cigarettes, the kind with five cigarettes to the pack. The last Buster had heard, the husband was still passing out cigarette samples at county fairs and sales meetings in West Virginia and Tennessee, but had graduated to Kents and menthol filter tips. His wife had made a novena every day since their daughter's elopement, offering up the plenary indulgences for her safe return, but they had never seen her again. Buster had lost his own faith at fourteen, but had found it useful to encourage his wife's infatuation with certain saints, as these dalliances allowed him not to pay much attention to her. It amused him that his wife was on such familiar terms with her saint of the moment. "As I said to Jack this morning," she would say; Jack was St. John Bosco and Frank was St. Francis de Sales. Her current litany was directed to "the Babe," which was her sobriquet for the Infant of Prague.

Buster had arrived in Las Vegas nine years before in the wake of a grand jury investigation of cor-

ruption in his police department. He had told his superiors that if he were on the take he would not be living
in a house in a changing neighborhood worth less than
when he bought it and that he would also be able to
afford a new automobile with the radio, heater and
automatic-shift options instead of the two secondhand
cars he owned, one with 37,000 miles on the odometer,
the other with 52,000 miles. If you want to ride someone into the slammer, Buster Mano told his superiors,
there's a detective third in the narco division cruising
around in a three-liter BMW. When his superiors insisted that he testify anyway, Buster resigned from the
department, took his lieutenant's pension of $412.97 a
month, plus the $7,000 in his savings account, and
moved to Vegas, where he opened a private investigator's agency. "If I'd been reached," he would say,
"I would have had a lot more than seven grand in the
savings account, and that's the truth. And I wouldn't
be living with a fruitcake that chats it up with Saint
Martin of Tours either."

But Buster was essentially a man without ran-
cor. He admired professionalism above all other vir-
tues, admired it equally on both sides of the law. "Gone
five years, never left a trace," he would say about a
missing person. "He's really a pro." Buster had come
to know Artha in a missing person's case. A husband
had come to Vegas for the Kelvinator convention and
had not gone home. His wife had located Buster in the
Yellow Pages and liked the sound of his name. She told
him that her husband's disappearance was part of a
pattern, that it had happened two years before, after the
convention in Miami, and five years before that at the
convention in Honolulu. She no longer bothered to

notify the police in the cities where the conventions took place. It would cost her two hundred dollars for Buster to find her husband and send him home to Kansas City, and the privacy was well worth the price to her. In Miami and Honolulu the trouble had begun with girls, and it was on this assumption that Buster began to look for the missing husband. His name was Al Fogelson and he was staying with the Kelvinator group at the Stardust. It took Buster just twelve hours to find that Al Fogelson had teamed up with Artha at the Stardust the last night of the convention. Artha's number was unlisted, but Buster got her address from a blackjack dealer named Fran McGraw who worked the graveyard shift at the Stardust. In cases like this there was always a lot left unsaid. The hotel wanted no trouble and Fran McGraw wanted to keep his job. Fran McGraw had graduated to the Strip after three years dealing twenty-one downtown on Fremont Street. The year before he had made $21,738, but had only paid income tax on $10,738. The rest he kept in his father's safe-deposit box. Fran McGraw had no checking account and only a minimal savings account. He had an old VW camper and lived west of the Strip in a two-bedroom apartment for which he paid $185 a month. There was no proof that Fran was cheating the Internal Revenue Service, but in his father's safe-deposit box there was close to $23,000 in fifties and hundreds. Fran's father kept the key to the box and there was no way he would let his son get at the money, because Fran was a gambler and his father wanted him to have a stake. Fran McGraw was not a compulsive gambler, one apt to blow $23,000 at a crack, but he was still capable of nibbling away at it three or four grand at a time. He did a little pimping on the side, never for money, just for free pussy and the tokes the johns gave him for lining up something for them. The johns were usually winners and wanted to close out the night with a piece of ass and sometimes could be counted on for a fifty- or even a hundred-dollar toke. Artha occasionally was on call from the pits at the Stardust, and that is how Fran McGraw had got to know her. He had never been to bed with her, although he kept on promising to treat himself to a free piece of ass, and sometimes he took Artha to see a movie. He always wanted her to beat him off in the movie, but Artha never did.

All these things were easy for Buster Mano to find out. He had a friend who was an IRS agent and he liked to drop the friend's name when someone was not being cooperative. It was Buster's opinion that everyone in Vegas was cheating on his income tax and the mere mention of his friend's name was enough to bring about total recall. Al Fogelson was last seen playing blackjack at Fran McGraw's table and Fran McGraw sometimes made introductions. It was as simple as that.

Once Buster Mano discovered Artha's address he drove to her apartment and waited outside. He did not go inside. That might have caused a scene and Buster hated scenes. He had a photograph of Al Fogelson and he knew that sooner or later Al Fogelson would come out. When Al Fogelson finally appeared carrying a load of dirty laundry, Buster followed him to the laundromat in Vegas Village. Al Fogelson was just stuffing his dirty underwear in a washing machine when Buster materialized at his side and told him it was time to go home. Al Fogelson did not seem surprised; he had been through the same thing in Miami and Honolulu.

There were no threats, no intimidation. Buster had only one job to do and that was to find the missing husband. He had done that and no more. If Al Fogelson went home to Kansas City, that was his business. If he did not, Buster would tail him for as long as Al Fogelson's wife wished. It was a job, a hundred dollars a day plus expenses. Buster had cleared $18,000 the year before, before taxes. He did not have $23,000 in his safe-deposit box, and that was why he was not averse to leaning on Fran McGraw just a little bit. Al Fogelson wanted to go back and say good-bye to Artha, but Buster persuaded him that as long as he was going home to KayCee anyway, perhaps it would be best to go direct to McCarran Airport. It was Buster's experience that hookers generally made a fuss when deprived of a mark and he did not like the idea of becoming known at Ralph Lamb's Sheriff's Department as the kind of private investigator who got involved in fusses.

Buster Mano himself drove Al Fogelson to McCarran International and when Al Fogelson was safely on board his plane, Buster called his wife and told her that her husband would arrive in Kansas City after a Denver stopover on United Flight 683. There was still the matter of Al Fogelson's suitcase. Buster told the wife that he could get it, but that it might cause a fuss. She said not to make a fuss, that her husband's return was sufficient. Al Fogelson had shaken Buster's hand as he departed on the flight to Denver and KayCee. "It was like I was his district sales manager," Buster Mano said.

Buster had found Al Fogelson even before he had a chance to deposit Mrs. Fogelson's two-hundred-dollar cashier's check into his bank account. Just to satisfy his own curiosity, he called the Kelvinator district sales manager and found out that the next year's convention was scheduled for New Orleans. "You want to know something?" Buster Mano said. "His wife will let him go." He liked to say that he was a student of human nature, that it was important in his job. "It gives her a sense of excitement," Buster said. "And it gives him something to feel guilty about." It was easy to explain. "Human nature," he said. "You've got to be a student of human nature in this job." Then he said that he had not made a bowel movement in two and a half days.

FOUR

Jackie Kasey was taking some steam. It was three P.M. on a Monday afternoon, he had a cold and he had done two shows the night before. Sunday night was a bad night for a lounge comic. The weekend mob had cleared out and the convention crowd was still settling in, getting their plastic name tags and drinking gin and orange juice or Seagram Seven and Seven in the hospitality suite. The insurance wives compared corsages and hair spray, their husbands the latest full-coverage floaters.

"Just tied up Ben Maddox."

"He still got that Chrysler-Plymouth agency over in Stockton?"

"No, sirree. He's into mobile homes. Ten thousand a whack."

"Discount pricing."

"And seven locations. New and used product. Newports, Vikings, Ramadas, all sizes and models."

"Synthetic shrubbery?"

"That's an extra. You know what his slogan is?"

"What's that?"

" 'The Mobile Home That Looks Like a Home.' "

"Good slogan."

"I think so."

All of which made the lounge comic's life more difficult. The convention crowd was not a high-rolling crowd in any case, and the first night in town they were too busy setting up prospects to look in on the lounges or to give the tables much play. The lounges were full only on weekends and so deserted the rest of the week that many of the hotels on the Strip were turning them into keno rooms. A keno room was open twenty-four hours a day and was therefore a profit center, much more so than an empty lounge where a $10,000-a-week comic spent Sunday to Thursday nights playing to audiences consisting mainly of hookers cruising for johns.

The empty house at the second show Sunday night had not made Jackie Kasey's cold any better. There was a black hooker with a gold left front tooth and a small American flag decaled to her bag working the bar and maybe forty other people scattered around a room that sat six hundred. The jokes just sat there.

"Why don't you all get at one table so I can talk to someone," Jackie said.

Nothing.

"One thing I found traveling around the country is that a night when no one is here you're in trouble."

Nothing.

•   •   •

The second show broke at two-thirty and Jackie wandered around the casino until five A.M. He was too revved up to go to bed and the cold was working its way down into his chest. This was his first shot as the head-liner in the lounge at the hotel and he had worked up a whole new act and the act was not going. He was forty years old and had spent twenty years working one-night stands at bowling alleys and smokers and automobile dealers' district sales meetings. He had learned his trade the hard way in places like the Chart House in Mil-waukee and Leo's Supper Club in Peoria, Illinois, and the Cool Club in Cairo and the Brentwood Country Club in Lexington, Kentucky. They were Mob joints mainly, with a line of girls out front and a private game in the back, and he worked on his Harold, the Homo Halfback routine and his Girl with the Itchy Twitchy routine and his Dangerous Dan, the Used Car Man routine. They went over big at the Pink Panther Room in Akron and the Club Capri in Cincinnati and the Aware Inn in Sioux City and Great Lakes Social Club in Buffalo, N.Y., but he flopped at the Copacabana in New York and was canceled out of the Town & Coun-try in Brooklyn after one night. He was doing a flamenco routine at the Town & Country and when he twirled his cape it knocked the wig off a woman sitting down front and the woman was the best friend of the boss's wife. He went back to club dates and worked out of Detroit and Miami and played four different spots a night in the Borscht Belt. He started in Vegas down-town on Fremont Street and then was the comedian in an ice show on the Strip, and then was signed to warm up for Frank and then for Dean, and then Colonel Tom Parker caught his act and hired him to warm up for

Elvis. He went on tour with Elvis and bought a house
in Beverly Hills, south of Wilshire, east of Doheny, but
still Beverly Hills, and the year before he had grossed
$108,000 and no one knew his name. Now he was hea-
dlining in the lounge at the hotel, he was making $10,-
000 a week, he had a cold, his act was not working and
there was still no one who knew his name.

Jackie got up early Monday afternoon, had
some breakfast and decided to take some steam for the
cold. He did not play golf, it was too hot to play tennis
and there was nothing else to do. The walls of the health
club were lined with autographed eight-by-ten glossies,
"To Lew Foxx, Best regards, Sandra Dee" and "To
Lew, One great guy, Roman Gabriel" and "To Lew,
Many thanks, Gene Tunney." Lew Foxx ran the health
spa. He was a very healthy pink-skinned man in his
mid-fifties, barrel-chested, with generous clumps of hair
growing out of his nostrils and creeping out of the back
of his shirt over the collar. He was not by trade a
masseur. He had once run some parking lots in Cleveland and was very well connected.

"What do you mean 'well connected'?"

"He knows some people."

"What people?"

"Guessssss," was the irritated reply, the all-pur-
pose Vegas reply when someone wished to imply a
connection with the People.

His connections had won Lew Foxx the health-
club franchise. He showed up at every opening night on
the Strip, sitting at a table down front with his wife, an
ex-Vegas show girl who was six inches taller than he
was. Or perhaps she was two inches shorter and had
eight inches more hair. Lew Foxx said that he was a

two-time loser before he met his present wife. Her name
was Valerie and he always referred to her as his "present wife."

"The first time I was just a kid," Lew Foxx said
about his first marriage. "I didn't know any better." His
second wife was someone his first wife caught him fooling around with when he was running the parking lots
in Cleveland. "I figured she was the cause for the divorce, I might as well marry her." The heel of his hand
slapped against his forehead. *"Oi veh."*

"I see what you mean, Lew."

"You know what my second wife used to do?"
Lew Foxx said. "She used to stick a pair of rosary beads
up my ass before I came. A broad does that you can
come for a week. She was a Catholic girl."

Jackie stripped and wrapped a towel around his
middle. The steam room at three P.M. Monday afternoon was full of middle-aged men with bad muscle tone
and good-sized tits, the kind that would cause a woman
to be described as small-breasted. The routine was un-
varying. Steam, sauna, whirlpool, Scotch douche, massage. In the Scotch douche, masseurs in white ducks,
white T-shirts and white shower clogs play high-
velocity hoses over the body, up one leg, down the
other, over the back muscles, down the arms and then
a playful stream at the privates. "Don't move," the
masseur would say, and the water would ease down the
stomach, stopping a safe couple of inches away from the
joint, then a quick squirt. "You moved."

"Jesus, you see him jump?"

"Lower and slower, Arnold."

"It may be small, but it's a willing little devil."

The conversation in the health club was slow

and desultory, as if each word were enveloped in the steam before it was released. The talk was of life and the community and it was the dialogue of the used-car tycoon and the parking-lot mogul.

"Joe E. Jason's going to warm up for Tom Jones."

"No kidding."

"Never made it in the lounge, Joe E."

"He's a hard man to employ, Joe. Not big enough to be a headliner, too big for a warm-up."

"He can only go with a headliner like Al Martino. Then he gets equal billing."

The muscles are kneaded, pounded, pushed into shape. Blow jobs are compared and private games in Chicago and Pittsburgh and Seattle.

"I went on a junket to London."

"Meet George Raft?"

"Sure I met George Raft."

"I heard about that junket. I heard one of the guys lost twenty-nine grand in a private game at the Mayfair. And he knew it was crooked."

"He just liked the action."

"I can understand that."

Silence, and then: "I knew a guy once in Gary, Indiana, and this guy, he called his root Jane. It's a funny name for a guy to call his joint, I mean, he wasn't a fairy or nothing, so I says to him, 'How come you call your root Jane?' And he says to me, 'I heard of a book once, it's called *Jane's Fighting Ships,* so I started to call my joint Jane.' "

"That makes sense."

Again the muscles are bruised into shape, the masseur's fingers pushing the pouches of fat up toward the shoulders, then smoothing them back down again.

"I did twenty-six shows over the weekend."

"No shit. What's the show?"

" 'Bowling With the Stars.' "

"You know something, I bet I've seen it."

"It's on all over. Syndicated."

"Peter Lawford, guys like that."

"Superstars."

"You know something, I never thought Peter Lawford bowled."

"Why's that?"

"He's English, right?"

"You figured him for tennis?"

"Right."

"That makes a lot of sense."

"I thought it did."

"So anyway, I put these twenty-six shows together over a weekend and I didn't have to take any time off for my publicity clients."

"You in publicity?"

"That's right."

"You know Mickey Rooney?"

"I know a lot of people who know him."

"I bet he's a nice guy."

"That's what I hear."

"You hear that, huh?"

"Yeah."

"That's nice to hear."

2

The first time I ever saw Jackie Kasey he was warming up for Elvis Presley. In the history of the

Strip, there had never been a bigger draw than Elvis. Right by the front door in the lobby, there was a booth set up to sell souvenirs of Elvis—records, pins, eight-by-ten glossies, even bumper stickers that read, VISIT ELVIS' BIRTHPLACE—TUPELO, MISSISSIPPI. The main room was packed tighter than a subway in a rush-hour summer thunderstorm, and the minimum was fifteen dollars a person, and for that fifteen dollars you got four drinks, which averaged out to $3.75 per Scotch whiskey, or a bottle of bilious California champagne, *pink* champagne which in the bizarre lighting in the International Ball Room turned an even more bilious lavender. And that was all you got because the room was too crowded for the waitresses, old girls with pencils stuck in their blue-tinted hair buns, to serve you any more, and so you were stuck with four drinks with all the ice melted even before the houselights went down.

It sometimes seemed to me that nothing so exactly expressed the feeling that Vegas was in a time warp as the appearance of Elvis on the Strip. The audience that first night I saw Jackie consisted mainly of the groupies of 1956, now thirty-some-year-old matrons with Alberto VO-5 bouffant hairdos and Empire dresses and strapless bras and gardenia corsages. It was hard to imagine that these matrons with the propped-up falsie tits were the same teenagers who a decade and a half earlier had torn off Elvis' clothes and traded in that photograph of him in *Life* magazine, the one with the succulent carbuncle decorating the middle of his back. Now they had husbands in the dental-supply game and kids who were not turned on to the thirty-five-year-old Elvis, kids who wanted to boff the lead guitarist in the Three Dog Night and who could not comprehend that their mothers were once pimple freaks.

It was a tough audience for a warm-up comic, and the job was already tough enough. The warm-up comic has forty-five minutes and functions basically as a high colonic, getting the audience through dinner, one trip to the john, a little juice on board, loosening them up for the headliner. He stands up there, a guy with six tuxedos in his closet, every one with the sky-blue lining, and he opens the tuxedo and gives the audience a hint of the lining and it looks like he's hustling After Six. He snaps the microphone cord as if it were a bullwhip, shoots out the pinky finger and launches a fusillade of one liners.

"Speaking of Italians . . . " He had not been speaking of Italians, but there is not a stand-up comic in Vegas who does not change his line of thought with the phrase, "Speaking of . . ."

"Speaking of Italians, they had birth control long before the pill." A beat. "They called it garlic." Another beat. "Even the Pope uses it."

The audience laughs, mechanically at first, then more appreciatively. The minutes are passing, the headliner is getting ready backstage, the creamed chicken has not started to react chemically with the crème de menthe parfait to block the lower intestinal tract.

"And speaking of Jews, I got so many caps on my teeth my mother's chicken soup bends my mouth."

Back and forth across the stage, the sweat soaking through the blue lining of the After Six. "And listen, you ever see a Jew schlepping with the football? The Jew is the team treasurer."

He is the liege of the star, funny but not too funny, the headliner must never be upstaged. "And look at the teams. Everyone is represented. Our Indian brothers—the Redskins. Our feathered friends—the Falcons. The fish in the sea—the Dolphins. Even the Commies—the Cincinnati Reds, right? What about the Jews? So why don't they call a team the Miami Beach Accountants or the Newark Optometrists?"

The dishes are being cleared away, it is time to go. "And speaking of fags, excuse me, laze and gemmen"—the voice becomes sibilant—"gay liberation it's called today. I'm a honkie, my brother-in-law's a pig, but I can't call a fag a fag. But speaking honestly, laze and gemmen, you know what the gay cathedral is called?" A beat. "St. Bruce's."

Time is up, the star awaits. "God love you, laze and gemmen, you've been a great audience." The two-handed kiss. "Peace and love, peace and love."

Upstairs to the second-floor dressing room, coated with sweat, temper out of sorts. "The headliner comes out, the people have finished their dinner. I come out, all I can hear is the waiters saying, 'You want the parfait or the mousse, the mousse is the soft stuff.' "

A quick shower, then three hours to the next show. Stomach in knots, can't eat, can't drink, can't nap, no time to fuck even except with a hooker and it is very tough to go back onstage after forty-eight minutes with a hundred-dollar hooker who washes your joint the first thing she does, no matter how many times she has been with you, and after something like that it is difficult to make with the jokes about the Miami Beach Accountants.

3

"Who wants to ball a spade hooker?" Jackie
Kasey said. He was standing in the lobby of the hotel,
a short man with dark crinkly hair, smelling of expensive toilet water and wearing a beige jump-suit ensem-
ble. It was after the second show Sunday night and I
was telling him about the black prostitute in the bar, the
one with the gold front tooth and the American flag
decal on her bag. She had been propositioning a trick
when I walked into the lounge where Jackie was playing, and without turning away from the prospective
john she had motioned me to the other stool beside her.
As I ordered a drink, she lit a cigarette, and from
behind her cupped hand she said to me, sotto voce, "I'm
just keeping you in the bull pen in case this one doesn't
work out." Dramatically blowing a smoke ring, she
then turned back to the other man and began negotiating price and specialties, the little gimmicks that would
make the time with her well spent. I heard her say that
the gold tooth ought to be worth something, she bet
that he had never been given head by a girl with a gold
front tooth. The man thought for a moment and then
said no, he guessed he hadn't.

All the while, Jackie had been up onstage,
sweating profusely, a very nervous man making $10,-
000 a week in his first headline appearance in the
lounge, but only playing harmony, it seemed from the
bar, to a hooker with a gold tooth. The few people in
the room for the second show were spread out instead
of all grouped down front, in order that each waitress
could get a crack at a tip. It did not at all improve
Jackie's disposition that the waitresses' tips were considered more important than an audience for him to

play against. He had worked up a new routine for his shot in the lounge. No more the stand-up comic in an After Six with a sky-blue lining. No more Harold, the Homo Halfback, no more Dangerous Dan, the Used Car Man. Jackie was a theme comic now: check that— a theme *comedian*. Corbett Monica and Pat Henry, they were comics, but a comedian dealt not in jokes but in *character*, a character who was *characterized*, a character with *characterization*, and the characterization gave the comedian what he never had before, and that was an *identity*, and what the identity did was make you *identifiable*, and if you were identifiable, you could be *marketed*, turned into a *product*.

First there was the overture from the gospel singers:

The product that Jackie Kasey hoped to become was Brother JayJay. Brother JayJay was an evangelist. Seedy, conniving, opportunistic, the epitome of likable low cunning, the major-domo of a moth-eaten Elmer Gantry tent show. Jackie had planned his wardrobe with extreme care. A tambourine, cheap rings covering every knuckle, a lavender silk frock coat and matching pants. Singing and clapping from a white-robed sisterhood of black gospel singers. The only trouble was the room was empty, there was no playback from the audience. That, and also the act was not very good, it needed work.

First there was the overture from the gospel singers:

> "Way down south
> In the land of cotton
> Brother Jay am not forgotten
> Here he come, here he come, here he come
> Brother Jay."

Clapping and hooraying from the gospel singers as Brother JayJay bounced on stage, a mendacious look in his eye:

"Thank you, sisters. Thank you, brothers. Thank you, saints. And hallelujah, you sinners. I'm partial to sinners—being no saint myself.
"But the good Lord loves the sheep who strays from the flock. And I stray so much I get an awful lot of loving."

"Amen, brother," said the gospel singers.

"You know, just last week I went to a sin-o-teria. In the interests of research, of course. I tried a little of everything—and a second helping of lust. YOU HEAR ME, LORD? YOU, THE CAT UP THERE WITH THE FUZZ ON YOUR FACE AND THE GROOVY WHITE CAFTAN."

"Amen, brother."

"Then I seen the error of my ways and decided to cleanse myself. They wanted to bathe me in the river, but ohhhh, that water was so cold. I went through a car wash instead. With the windows up. Got the soul and the white walls done in one operation."

"Amen, brother."

It was like a revival played to an empty tent. I watched fascinated from the bar. Watching a comic flailing against an indifferent audience seemed a refraction of my own depression. Vegas has a way of co-opting burned-out cases; there is a sense that failed expectations are the mean, the norm. Here was a jester to the affluent proletariat; here was comedy essentially prejudiced, not in the racial sense, but in reinforcing resistance to change. It seemed no accident that kings employed jesters; they deflated individual pretensions, deviations from established values.

I felt the hooker's hand slide over mine. The prospective trick had left, ostensibly for the men's room, but he had not returned. He had left a full drink and a freshly opened package of Larks.

"I guess he never went with no colored girl," she said. She tapped her glass against her gold tooth. "You want to date?"

I assured her I wished to remain in the bull pen.

She picked up his Larks. "I'll trade you these for your Salems. I like menthol."

The exchange was made. She beckoned the bartender. "He pay for my drink?"

The bartender shook his head.

"The cocksucker," she said pleasantly. She patted my hand. "Settle it for me, honey," she said. "And dream about what you're missing." And then she was gone.

In the lobby after the show, Jackie Kasey was unimpressed by my account of the black hooker. "What was she, some kind of Watusi with the gold tooth?" The vowels were all flattened out, the diction slightly nasal. He wore glasses offstage. "Twenty dollars and a catheter up your cock. Stick with the white stuff."

His eyes roamed the casino restlessly. There were brochures of Brother JayJay scattered about the lobby and he checked every location to make sure that the supply was not running out. His conversation was manic, like a nonstop LP. He had a tendency to exaggerate in the most meaningless manner. He would try a story out on me, then repeat it slightly changed a few seconds later, as if I had rematerialized before him tabula rasa, and then with a slight change of emphasis a third time. "You know, there's these nuns staying at the hotel and they thought I was an evangelist."

"They come in the lounge and see your act?"

"No, you see there's these nuns in the hotel and they asked this bellhop if there was an evangelist staying here."

He dropped a Brother JayJay brochure into every empty chair in the lobby. "You see, there's these nuns here and they asked the bellhop why an evangelist was holding a revival in the hotel."

The story seemed to satisfy him now. "They wanted to know who this Brother JayJay was, you know, what church he belonged to. I guess they wanted to come to the meeting, you know, in their nun's suit."

It was nearly four A.M. and he bounded across the casino, stopping at each table, saying, "You wanna be saved, sister? I is Brother JayJay. The Lord may be your shepherd, but Brother JayJay says you stay with a soft seventeen."

He settled into a chair in the Persian Bar, clapping his hands for a drink. "Honey, I'll have a Scotch and soda pop-a-lop-a-dop and a couple of cube-a-loob-boobs, heavy on the bevy, the light kind." The double talk was something he used with strangers and menials, almost as a way of making connections. Out of my own inertia I found myself carried along on the pointless tide of his compulsion to connect.

He rattled on, his conversation a compendium

of triumphs, story after story about best friends who had to step aside and watch him rise, because that was the nature of the business, friends who did not have it on nights when he did. I watched and said nothing, with a rising sense of exhilaration that I was onto a good thing, the $10,000-a-week never-was and never-will-be, and I tried not to think how ultimately I would use him.

"Like with Frank at the Riviera. That's when it all started, that's where I busted through. Frank was my best friend and I was opening up for him. I mean, he said he wouldn't go to the Riv unless I was on the bill with him. And I left him for dead. A standing ovation on opening night. I mean, how could he follow a standing ovation."

Trying to interrupt was like trying to hold back a tidal wave with a sieve. He would stare open-mouthed as if I had been speaking Urdu, eyes dead, jaw slack, then he would snap his finger at a waitress. "Dis is Brudda JayJay, you wanna be saved?"

The waitress was balloon-bosomed. "Amen, Brother JayJay."

Benediction with a leer. "I do my saving in Room 2529."

"Oh, Jackie."

Again the double-talk order for another drink. "You see what I mean?" Jackie Kasey said. "You got to get the little people behind you. The waitresses and the bartenders. They talk about you, the little people. They tell the customers to come to the show. You can't make it in Vegas without the little people."

It was as if he were talking about a serving class of three-foot-two midgets.

"The thing about Brother JayJay, he can be marketed. You know, like a product. T-shirts, records,

Brother JayJay games. Dolls, balloons, not just the saloons, into the stores. A product. Lunch boxes, diaries,
comic books. You ever heard of Monopoly? It's a game.
We can do something like that with Brother JayJay's
land company or Brother JayJay's insurance company.
Fun things."

It was nearly five in the morning and it did not
seem the time to talk about the apathy of the audience
at the second show. "I got to take a leak," he said.

He burst through the door of the men's room,
dismayed at first because there was no attendant, no one
at whom to fire a joke, no one to ask if he wanted to be
saved. He stood in front of the urinal, unzipping his
beige jump suit; he practically had to undress to take a
leak. "It's not easy being a semi-name," he said, flexing
his knees in front of the urinal. "You got to wear shit
like this."

He peed generously, flexed his knees again and
rezipped. "I hate dribblers," he said. "I like guys who
really take a piss. Show me a guy who dribbles down
the side of his pants and I'll show you a loser, I'll show
you a guy who three-putts his way through life. You got
to give it a good shake."

He washed his hands like a surgeon scrubbing
for an operation, the soap easing over the manicure into
the cuticles, the suds thick and enticing. Then the rinse,
hands under the hot water until the steam rose. He
wiped his hands, looked into the mirror and blew himself a kiss off his wrinkled fingers.

"There is nothing," Jackie Kasey said, "like a
good piss."

FIVE

ime took on a kind of pattern. For days on end I did not leave the apartment. I subsisted on a diet of Clark bars and Hydrox cookies and Hostess Twinkies and, when I was feeling flush, cans of macadamia nuts. I drank Coca-Cola out of deposit bottles because I was sure that the taste in the no-return bottles was different, sweeter, not so much carbonation. I ate Neccos, the little host-like candy wafers, and Oreos and Florentine Pogens. I ate cube steak and Macintosh apples and Ritz crackers with Laura Scudder crunchy peanut butter.

I got fat.

I received a letter in the mail one day from a man in Cincinnati. We had never met, he had never read anything I had written, but he knew my address at the Royal Polynesian Apartments. He said he had seen my picture in a magazine and that he was deeply into ESP. He wanted to tell me that he foresaw terrible things happening to me over the next three months. He did not say what terrible things. Just terrible things. I wondered how he had got my address. Probably ESP.

There was a return address on the letter, but I did not write back. I did not wish to know what terrible things were in store.

But I wondered. Death? Disfigurement? Suicide? Scratch suicide.

The summer heat burned into the cortex of the brain. It was something tangible, hallucinogenic, dipping under a hundred degrees only after midnight, so hot outside that a heat headache seemed a permanent, terminal condition. Even the rain was no release. It was obscurely unsettling to watch the thermometer in the tower clock of the Sahara blinking 112° through the rain. The wind blew, a hot dry wind like a fire storm, banging the warm lumps of rain against the windows of my apartment. Everything in the Royal Polynesian seemed to creak and groan under the weight of the blow, as if the construction joints were coming asunder. The rain clanged against the metal porch furniture on my terrace like so many rounds of buckshot, and in the vacant lot behind my apartment the sand and the tumbleweed were whipped into what seemed a crazed war dance.

Only the air conditioning subverted the tyranny of the weather. In the summer one becomes a slave in Vegas to the vagaries of hydroelectric power; from dawn to dawn the air one breathes is not off the Nevada desert but the artificial cooling generated by the turbines of Hoover Dam. There was Muzak piped into the apartment, Mantovani and the Melachrino Strings, and I played the radio all day. I grew fond of a call-in program with hints for homemakers.

"The thing is this, Barry, what I wanted to ask you about . . ."

"Shoot, Tina."

"I told you I've got this kind of aqua brocade living-room suite, you know, blue-green?"

"Right, Tina. Aqua."

"So my problem is . . . we've got the light-green walls, right?"

"I think I see your problem, Tina."

"It's . . . you know, kind of dull?"

"Accent colors. You need accent colors. Pillows. You ladies probably think I've got some kind of *pillow* franchise, I mention them so often, but . . ."

"Right, Barry. I remembered the pillow idea. But, uh, Barry, what color pillows?"

The Muzak segued from "Ebbtide" into "The Theme from Moulin Rouge." The news programs on the radio were a recitative of automobile accidents.

"Outside Tonapah last night, a Dodge camper overturned on Highway Six. Esmeralda County sheriff's department officials estimate the vehicle was traveling at a rate of speed of ninety miles per hour when it apparently hit a coyote crossing the highway. The victims were identified this morning as Dale John Ewing, seventeen, and Eulene McKee, thirty-eight, both of Basalt."

Back to homemaking hints.

"Listen, Barry, I bought this settee at Levitz . . ."

"No brand names, Linda."

"Sorry, Barry, I thought Levitz was a sponsor."

"Why don't you just call it a name-brand settee, Linda?"

"That's a good idea, Barry."

Nothing more important occupied my mind

than what Dale John, seventeen, had been doing in Tonapah with Eulene, thirty-eight. A tryst? A mattress in the back of that Dodge camper? A six-pack of Coors and a tumble in the desert? It made the hours pass to wonder.

For a long time the only person I saw was Jackie. It was a friendship corrupted by a knowledge that I did not share with him, a knowledge that he was a great character, a character to be cultivated like a rare orchid. If I had not found Jackie, I doubt that I would have stayed long in Vegas. And so I nurtured him, exchanging confidences, opening doors into the darkest alcoves of my life, creating in him a trust I knew I would ultimately violate. He became expansive, opened up; I took notes and felt badly about it. We went everywhere together. One afternoon I took some steam with him. In the sauna two naked men were discussing their physical condition.

"I go to this place in New York. You check in for three days and they got a finger up your ass the whole time."

"I heard they do that."

"And then every three months you send them a stool sample so they can analyze it."

"A stool sample?"

"That's right. And don't say 'No shit.' "

"How'd you know I was going to say that."

"I just knew."

"You're right, I was."

"You put it in a plastic baggie and send it to them in the mail."

"A plastic baggie, is that right?"

"That's what I said. And they can look at that
stool and they can almost tell if you got the clap."

"They send it back to you."

"No, they keep it. You just get the results."

"You can't send dirty books through the mail,
but you can send a piece of shit."

"That's right."

"This fucking government."

Afterward I walked with Jackie on the Mezza-
nine Mecca of the hotel, past the swimming pool, tennis
courts and an Astro-turf putting green. The Mecca was
crowded with mottled men with hair on their stomachs
and reflectors parked under their copious chins and
with wives and girl friends who seemed to have mod-
eled their looks and life styles on Virginia Hill or the
Andrews Sisters. A female employee of the hotel was
giving a guided tour of the Mecca to a group of Girl
Scouts.

Jackie spotted the Girl Scouts and was immediately on, always the shill for his own act. "I don't want
no cookies, I don't want no cookies," he said in a
parody of a child's voice. "I had your tollhouse cookies
and you Girl Scouts are trying to poison me. You put
poison in your chocolate bits. I know you Girl Scouts,
I know your type."

The Girl Scouts looked as if they had been confronted by a Martian. "Who's he?" one finally asked the
tour guide.

"That's Jackie," the tour guide said. She had a
face as vacant as a creature in a wet dream. Her breasts
were like isosceles triangles and the bulbs of her buttocks leaked out from under her shorts.

"Jackie who?" the Girl Scout said.

"Jackie the comedian."

"Oh," the Girl Scout said. The Scout motto, "Be Prepared," was stitched on the arm of her uniform, and I wondered, Prepared for what, prepared for the Mecca? Were these nubiles in their green uniforms and their green berets, offspring of pit bosses and blackjack dealers, backbone of Las Vegas' schools and churches, really prepared for men with hair on their stomachs who sent their shit back east air express in plastic baggies, prepared for a tour guide with a face devoid of sexual content, prepared for a comic in a blue knit jump suit prattling baby talk?

It seemed a lunatic joke. The joke, however, passed Jackie by. The Girl Scouts might not know him, but still he was on, dancing among the swimmers and sunbathers, threading his way through the beach towels and the Bain de Soleil and the silver reflectors, repeating the manic refrain, "You wanna be saved, you wanna be saved?"

The sunbathers seemed perplexed at this Malamudian mite with the saucy little tennis hat perched on the top of his head. "You wanna be saved?" From what? A man's in Vegas, his stomach's glistening with suntan oil, he's $4,200 ahead and looking for a little baccarat action tonight, his stools are winging toward the Big Apple in a 747, and this mad little runt in a blue knit jump suit and a saucy little tennis hat is trotting around the pool knocking the Sea & Ski over onto the pages of *The Love Machine* and saying, "You want to be saved?" It was enough to make a man lose his faith in Vegas.

"The lounge. Ten-fifteen."

SIX

Marvin Berlin talking:

"How'd I come to Vegas? On a Greyhound bus with a fine old derby.

"No, seriously, I'll tell you what happened. I had a photo studio in Los Angeles on Sunset Boulevard. A monstrous big place. You know where the Mercedes-Benz showroom is today? Between Wilcox and Cahuenga? That was my photo studio.

"I'd shoot record-album covers, that kind of stuff, and I'd just about keep my head above water. I used to go down to Norm's, that's a coffee shop, to get my lunch. I'd go down to Norm's at a dead run so I wouldn't waste any time, and every day, there was this man standing outside. He looked like Alfred Hitchcock. And he said, 'I always see you running back and forth.'

"And I said, 'I'm down at my photo studio. I just got time to grab a sandwich to go.'

"And he said, 'You must be making nine tons of money down there.'

"And I said, 'I'm making one ton of money and I've got eight tons of bills.'

"And he said, 'I never would have thought it.'

"And I said, 'Listen, if you want to talk, I got some prints in the wash, come back and we'll discuss.'

"And so he comes back to my photo studio with me. And he says, 'You know, if you're not making any money with this kind of overhead, you're crazy.'

"And I said, 'So what should I do?'

"And he said, 'You should go to Vegas and become a dealer.'

"And I said, 'How come *you* don't go to Vegas to become a dealer?'

"And he said, 'I suffer from anxiety neurosis. It used to be called shell shock. I can't stand the pressure, I start shaking, I get a partial pension for it.'

"And I said, 'Is it really that good in Vegas?'

"And he said, 'It's really that good. You know what I'd like to do?'

"And I said, 'What would you like to do?'

"And he said, 'I'd sure like to open up a dealing school here in Los Angeles. If only I could get a license.'

"And I said, 'Why'd they refuse your license?'

"And he said, 'They didn't. I never applied.'

"And I said, 'Why don't you apply? You might get a surprise.'

"So he applied and they gave him a license and he'd come into my photo studio and he'd say, 'I'm going to teach you how to deal.' He was on a saving-people-from-themselves kick and he was going to rehabilitate me, get me out of debt. And so he taught me how to deal. He really did. Then some time later I was ass-deep in debt and I closed the photo studio and came to Vegas. As a dealer."

It was twelve noon and the school day was just beginning at the Casino Dealers School, Inc. Marvin Berlin sat at his desk and watched the students trail in, many of them out of work, victims of the recession that was gripping Vegas as well as the rest of the nation, a former tumbler, a youth with a dog act, a carpenter laid off at Nellis Air Force Base, most of them men with duck's-ass haircuts and acne-pitted faces, but a few women as well, heavy in the haunches, pinched and strained around the eyes and mouth. He was a spruce little man, Marvin Berlin, with a trim mustache and a Cockney accent, bald on top and a neat fringe over the ears. He had this romantic notion of himself as a dealer-photographer, a hyphenate, and he had worked down-town on Fremont Street and he had worked all over the Strip, the Flamingo, the Dunes, Circus Circus, and when the mood struck him he would go off to Spain for the summer or to Oregon to shoot the big trees. He had eight prints hanging in a gallery in Carmel and there was a one-man exhibit of his photos scheduled for a show right here in Vegas. He was out of dealing now and into teaching and his school was over a kosher restaurant on Las Vegas Boulevard North. The hours on the floor of the casino were too long and he had a color lab in his house and all his cameras and equipment were paid for and the school gave him more time to prepare for his one-man show.

He had one roulette table, two crap tables and six blackjack tables and some forty students who received at the end of their 130 hours' instruction a diploma that said,

CERTIFICATE
CASINO DEALERS SCHOOL
John Doe
Has Completed His Course
In Dealing Crap As A
Qualified Dealer.
Marvin Berlin
President.

Marvin Berlin told me that the school was approved for veterans.

Marvin Berlin talking:

"The first thing I do when a student arrives, someone who wants to be a crap dealer, someone who has never been exposed to any casino action before, is give him two stacks of checks—that's what we call chips in this business—and teach him how to count them the way a dealer does. I keep him doing it until he gets some kind of facility with his fingers. Now, this can be deadly monotonous, so I'm also teaching him the layout of the table, what the winners are, what the losers are, and the procedures of picking up the losing bets and paying off the winning bets. And all the while he's getting some dexterity with his fingers. Good hands, that's the important thing."

"What about roulette?"

"The first thing you do there is teach the student how to spin the ball. That looks very easy, but if you don't know what you are doing, the ball is going to go straight up into the air and never come back, which could be very embarrassing."

"And blackjack?"

"Well, with blackjack, I teach the student card delivery first. And also how to handle the checks. It's a little different than handling the checks in crap because with blackjack you've got the deck of cards in one hand. So I teach him shuffling with one deck, double decks and four decks out of a shoe, which a lot of casinos are using these days. Now different casinos require different methods of dealing. Some want the dealers to turn over the cards and pay as they go. Some want them to turn over all the players' cards and then pay. The most difficult way is to pick and pay as you go."

"Once a student graduates, is it hard for him to get a job in a casino?"

"It depends."

"On what?"

"It helps if he has some juice."

"What's juice?"

"I guess you'd call it pull. Or clout."

"It's important."

"Vegas runs on juice. You sometimes hear someone say 'I've got more juice than Minute Maid.' That means he's got friends."

"What kind of friends?"

"In Vegas, it's best not to inquire."

"So if you've got juice, you can get a job?"

"Let's say it doesn't hurt. The easiest game to deal is blackjack, so that's where someone with the right connections can get a job easiest. You find that most blackjack dealers have a little juice. Maybe not so much as Minute Maid, but some."

"The same with craps?"

"Not so much, no. Craps is the toughest game to learn. You've got to know your onions to deal craps. The odds, the propositions, how to compute the payoffs on bets, the simple bets, the not-so-simple bets, the place bets, pass, don't pass, the field and so on. Someone with a little juice and not many brains can deal blackjack. But no brains and a lot of juice is going to hurt the house dealing craps. There's too many payoffs for too many combinations. If you've got juice and you're smart, you're okay. If you've got juice and you're dumb, you're in another line of work."

"What about baccarat?"

"Baccarat is played with cash on the table and no chips. A two-thousand-dollar limit. That's a lot of cash on the table."

"So you need a lot of juice to deal baccarat?"

"To deal baccarat you've got to be a nephew of the Godfather."

2

I met Marvin Berlin the way I met everyone in Vegas: I called him on the telephone. I talked for hours on the telephone, mainly to kill time, but also to encourage the self-delusion that I was working, that I was getting a feel of the community, that I was surfeiting myself with local color. The telephoning had the same narcotic effect as driving the freeways. I studied the Yellow Pages as if they were the key to the universe, and then would dial an accordion instructor or an abdominal-support salesman. I talked to exterminators and contraceptive wholesalers, bail bondsmen and private detectives. I slept fitfully, an hour here, two hours there, masturbating frequently, trying to find the release for sleep. I had insomnia and in the gray hours before dawn I could hear the whistle of a train, a freight ninety, a hundred cars long, snaking across the desert on the tracks behind Circus Circus. I had not heard the sound of a freight since my childhood summers in Saybrook, Connecticut. I belonged to a different generation. In Los Angeles, I used to go to the airport Sunday mornings to buy *The New York Times* and then park the car at the end of Runway No. 1 while the jets screeched over, not fifty feet above the road, the screech of the engines loud enough to puncture the eardrums. One had no perspective there at the foot of Runway No. 1, and each jet seemed as if it would plow right through the Firebird. It was a kind of safe death wish, like trying to cut your wrists with an electric razor, a possibility but not a likelihood.

I felt like an electronic Mr. Lonelyhearts. At three or four in the morning, people were somehow amenable to talking to a stranger on the telephone. Before dawn one morning I called an all-night drugstore that was advertising a special—1,000 prophylactics for the price of 750. "Any takers?" I said.

"You the press or something?"

"No, I just can't sleep. Saw the sign when I was buying some Crest yesterday. Interesting."

"Can't give them away."

"Really?"

"You got to be an optimist."

"You think?"

"Jesus, buddy, that's three years of steady popping. You know anybody who's popped every day the last three years, you just send him in."

"Come to think of it, I don't know anybody."

"Exactly."

"What brand?"

"Sheiks."

"Used Sheiks when I was a kid."

"Didn't use Rameses?"

"No."

"I was a Rameses man myself."

"Rameses," I said. "I'll be damned."

There was a long pause. "Anything more I can help you with?"

"I'd like a toothbrush," I said.

"What kind?"

"I've heard good things about Oral-B."

"We stock them," he said. But I could not engage him in any more conversation. I considered calling a dentist to discuss toothbrushes, plaque and preventive dentistry, but resolved to wait until morning.

The daytime calls were generally of a more serious nature. From the Chamber of Commerce I had picked up a catalog of the University of Nevada, Las Vegas, and as I was thumbing through it I discovered under "Campus Organizations (Religious)" that the Roman Catholic Newman Club was listed as the "Neumann Club." I placed a call to the UNLV publicity department. "I'm interested in your Neumann Club," I said.

"The what?"

"The Neumann Club."

"I'm not aware of any Neumann Club."

"It's in the catalog."

"Let me check." He returned to the phone after

several moments. "The Catholic group."

"Church of Rome, yes."

"What about it?"

"It's named after John Henry Newman, right?"

"I don't know anyone of that name."

"Cardinal Newman."

"It could be."

"He spelled it N-E-W-M-A-N."

"We spell it N-E-U-M-A-N-N."

"Why's that?"

"Could be named after a different fellow."

"You a Catholic?" I said.

"Christian Science."

"Mary Baker Eddy," I said.

"That's right."

"E-D-D-I-E?"

"E-D-D-Y."

"N-E-W-M-A-N."

The phone clicked in my ear.

3

I met Maisy Morgan in the pursuit of her profession as a practicing graphologist. Maisy Morgan. Real name Maureen Moran. Thirty-four years old. Former show girl in the line at the Tropicana. That was the season her name occasionally appeared in Ramsey Tait's column as being seen in the big room at the Riviera with someone in on a New Orleans junket. Maisy Morgan did not much like people from New Orleans. They drank too much and when they were drunk they would sometimes ask her to beat them off under the tablecloth in the big room while the show was going on. Maisy Morgan thought this was disrespectful to her and also to the act on stage. She liked to say that she stood in awe of talent. Not that she had been struck dumb by any of the talent she had met in her season in the line at the Tropicana. There had been a comic in the lounge who had promised to marry her and after she had driven to Nogales and had the abortion she discovered that the comic already had a wife in both Pittsburgh and St. Louis. The trip to Nogales had cost her the job in the line at the Tropicana because she had started to hemorrhage and had to stay in bed for a couple of weeks and when she got back to Vegas the job was gone. In the past she had occasionally spent weekends with people in on a junket when she needed money, so she free-lanced along the Strip for a while until the new Lido de Paris Revue started holding auditions. The creator of the Revue had once told her that she had the best nipples on the Strip, perky even when she was not getting laid, whereas most of the girls on the line had to rub ice cubes on their nipples to get them up before a show. Maisy Morgan was sure her nipples would get her a job in the Lido de Paris Revue, but then one morning she noticed a lump on her left breast and two weeks later she had a mastectomy.

Maisy Morgan never thought much about having one breast, although sometimes when she was drunk she said she thought it was "freaky." She was twenty-six years old when she had the mastectomy and her condition was conducive neither to working in a line nor to free-lancing. Whenever someone wanted to ball her, Maisy Morgan would carefully tell him that he was only getting half of what he expected up top, and if that did not bother him she would be honored to go to bed with him. In matters sexual, Maisy Morgan always affected a rococo speaking style. It was this manner of speech which had first attracted Dominick DiCicco, that and the fact, as he told Maisy Morgan later, that "fucking a girl with one tit was a first for old Dom." Dominick DiCicco was Maisy Morgan's second husband and she had not seen him in seven years. Maisy Morgan had married the first time when she was fifteen and seven months pregnant. Her first husband's name was Eugene Pruitt and Eugene had not been inclined to marry Maisy when she told him that she had missed three months in a row. Eugene Pruitt was the high scorer on the Green City, Oklahoma, basketball team, which in 1957 had gone to the semi-finals in the Class B state tournament. Even today, Maisy Morgan would recall, there was still a faded sign on the outskirts of Green City, Oklahoma, that had been erected by the Chamber of Commerce and that said, "Welcome to Green City, Home of the Green Hornets, 1957 Class B Semi-Finalists, Oklahoma Interscholastic Basketball Tourney."

Eugene Pruitt had been able to persuade the four other Green Hornet starters, plus two substitutes, that they all had had a whack at Maisy Morgan, a claim that Maisy said was not even half accurate. But Maisy Morgan's father had been able to convince Eugene Pruitt to marry his daughter with a promise of a half interest in his Phillips 66 station, that plus the vow to break Eugene Pruitt's legs with a tire iron if he did not do so. Maisy and Eugene were married in Carterville, Oklahoma, in March of 1957 with Maisy's father in attendance. Two days after the wedding, Eugene Pruitt

left Green City, Oklahoma, and enlisted in the United
States Marine Corps. Maisy Morgan's son was born in
St. Augustine's Hospital in Tulsa and she named him
Ralph, after her father. The child had six toes on each
foot and only one arm and died four days after birth.
Maisy called it a blessing. She never told Eugene Pruitt
of either the birth or death of her son, although she was
reasonably sure that he was the father. Eugene was
killed on the beach during the invasion of Lebanon in
1958. It was not of course a combat situation, but Eugene, who had risen to the rank of lance corporal, had
slipped in the sand and was run over by an amphibious
half-track, which had crushed his spine. Eugene Pruitt
was one of five Americans killed in the entire Lebanese
operation.

    Now that she was thirty-four and had only one
breast and was a practicing graphologist, Maisy Morgan was less interested in Ramsey Tait than in Dr.
Alvarez and Ann Landers. Every morning between
nine and eleven, she would saturate her Nescafé with
Coffeemate and saccharin and settle down to see what
Dr. Alvarez had to say about Pap smears. Maisy Morgan had a Pap smear every six months and her
gynecologist, who attended all the name female acts on
the Strip, mainly because of his philanthropy in dis-
pensing reds, had told her she had nothing to worry
about. But Maisy's absent breast often itched and the
itching would make her think of Bartholin abscesses,
and she would scour Dr. Alvarez to see what he had to
say about vaginal disorders. Maisy no longer used a
contraceptive because she was convinced that the mastectomy protected her from ever again becoming pregnant. She readily admitted that this was a superstition

without much basis in medical fact, but she said, "If you had had a kid with six toes on each foot, then I guess you'd be superstitious, too."

I readily agreed that I would be superstitious too. It was nearly five in the morning and Maisy Morgan and I were sitting in the coffee shop at Caesars Palace. I was constantly amazed in the months that I was in Vegas by the encounter-group atmosphere prevailing in the bars and coffee shops of the casinos during the hour or two before dawn. Here in this anteroom of purgatory was a constituency of the emotionally dispossessed. It was as if the end was at hand and there was only one priest to hear all the confessions.

The first thing that Maisy Morgan had said about my handwriting was that I had "original ideas." I am sure she had said this because she could not decipher my signature and had asked me to write down something longer, something that would give her more opportunity to decode the swirls and pressure points of my script. I was pretentious enough to jot down a few lines from Yeats:

> . . . *love is the crooked thing,*
> *There is nobody wise enough*
> *To find out all that is in it.*

"You have such original ideas," Maisy Morgan had said. I was not altogether sure whether she found them in the handwriting or in the Yeats. "You're artistic, you dislike routine and you're a nonconformist."

Which was why I was on my sixth cup of coffee at Caesars with her, awaiting the arrival of her new boy friend, Sonny Silver. Writers, she had said, were good listeners, and she had filled me in on the mastectomy while polishing off the pastrami on pumpernickel.

"You're going to like Sonny," she said. "I read his hand and knew right away that he was in some kind of athletics. You could tell."

You certainly could. Sonny Silver was four feet nine and three-quarter inches tall and was an ex-jockey. He worked for one of the biggest comedians on the Strip as a combination gofer, masseur, bookie and pimp. His profession was unique to Vegas; he was a sidekick. He had been the sidekick to a singer before the comic and to one of the People before that. He made them laugh, he knew where to get a knish at five in the morning or that the fifth at Hollywood Park was a boat race or that there was a hooker on the Strip who would pop her glass eye and take it in the socket.

"How you hitting them, slugger," he said when we shook hands. He pointed to Maisy Morgan. "She tell you about the boob?"

I did not quite know what to say.

"She tells everyone about that tit. You know, I think she's really looking for it. She's going to be driving down the Strip one night and here's this tit walking out the front door of the Desert Inn. With Howard Hughes. The first time anyone's seen Howard in forty-two years. But I knew Howard in the old days and if there's one thing he could never pass up it was a good tit."

Maisy Morgan was slapping the table, shaking with mirth. "Sonny, you really make me laugh."

"You know, I could have made it in a big room," Sonny Silver said. "But you got to be five feet tall. I defy you to name me one comic under five feet tall."

"Mickey Rooney."

"Five two and three-eighths."

Sonny Silver ordered a Shirley Temple. He said he never drank hard liquor. The comic he worked for was a heavy boozer and Sonny said it was up to him to be a good example. The comic billed Sonny Silver as "Entertainment Coordinator."

"People ask me what an entertainment coordinator is," Sonny Silver said, "and you know what I tell them?" He cupped his hand over the side of his mouth. " 'How much does the chick cost?' "

"Sonny, show John your trick," Maisy Morgan said.

"You want to see my trick?"

"Sure."

"Then I'll show you my trick."

Sonny Silver reached into his jacket and drew out a long sheet of lined paper. On the top of the paper he wrote down the number 68,000.

"Sixty-eight thousand, Sonny," Maisy Morgan said. "It was only sixty-six thousand this morning."

"It's been a good day, champ," Sonny Silver said. He mentioned the comic. "We had the house de-bugged. You know, half this town is wired. My friend and I, we make a lot of bets around the country. I know people at all the tracks. They say, 'Maisy's Tit in the fourth,' so we get a little action down. Eight to one, that's thirty-two grand at Del Mar alone. The feds know that, so they put a wire on your phone. I tell my friend I know a guy who can find the wire. So he comes in, finds the wire and for a couple of days you don't have the eagle on your ass. You get the eagle on your ass in this country, and you are in big trouble. The bastards ruined Dick Haymes. It wasn't Rita Hayworth, it was the eagle. All the eagle wants to do is put you in the slam."

"You better start, Sonny," Maisy Morgan said.

Sonny Silver took a gold pencil from his pocket. He said it was a personal gift from Sammy Davis, Jr. On the sheet of paper he began to write down numbers: 1, 2, 3, 4, 5, 6, 7, 8, 9, 10, 11. Maisy and I watched silently, trying not to interrupt Sonny Silver's concentration. The minutes passed. Sonny Silver wrote on, occasionally shaking his wrist to ward off writer's cramp. The numbers piled up on the paper. 434, 435, 436, 437. Ten minutes. Fifteen. Twenty. No one said a word. Finally, with a triumphant flourish, Sonny Silver wrote 69,000 at the bottom of the back side of the paper.

"I bet you never seen anything like that in your life," Sonny Silver said.

I still was not quite sure what I had just spent twenty-two minutes watching.

"I counted to a thousand," Sonny Silver said.

"Why?"

"Because I'm counting to a million."

"Oh."

"I bet you never met anyone in your whole life who's counted to a million."

"No."

"I've done it three times."

"That means that Sonny's counted to three million, if you add it all up," Maisy Morgan said.

"I guess that's what it means," I said.

"It's a very simple operation," Sonny Silver

said. "I take Sammy Davis' pencil here and three times a day I count up to a thousand."

"That's three thousand a day," Maisy Morgan said.

"I write it all down just so I got a record of it. You know, there's people in this town, you tell them you've counted to a million, they won't believe you."

"Yeah, I can believe that," I said.

"Takes about twenty minutes to a half-hour every time I count to a thousand. I write the number I begin with at the top of the page, the number I end with at the bottom. To double-check, so to speak."

I nodded.

"Any more than three times a day, you tend to lose interest," Sonny Silver said. "Less than that, the whole operation would take too long."

"You wouldn't want that."

"Did it once in three hundred thirty-three days. The longest was three hundred forty-five days. And I got a record of every page. Signed with the date. You want to witness this one?"

I signed my name with Sammy Davis' gold pencil on the page full of numbers. I asked what he did with the pages.

Sonny Silver said he gave them to the comic. "It makes him laugh. He shows them to real superstars. Buddy Hackett. Frank Gorshin."

"It really makes them laugh," Maisy Morgan said. "I've seen them."

"And people ask what an entertainment coordinator does," Sonny Silver said.

SEVEN

Ihad never met a private detective, which is why I called Buster Mano. He asked my name and where I was staying and then made an appointment for the following morning. His office was downtown, near the courthouse, on the ground floor of a parking garage, two rooms and the smell of small tragedy and petty defeat, of insignificant adultery and unpaid bills. There were two desks, some old copies of *Look,* a water cooler and a framed letter of appreciation from the Las Vegas Police Department in the outer office, and in the inner office, Buster's room, a refrigerator, a shotgun, a holstered revolver, a rifle stock on which was fitted a Nikon with a 600 mm lens, and a wooden bust of John F. Kennedy.

"Nice place, the Royal Polynesian," Buster Mano said. He was making instant coffee on the hot plate, which was under a huge photo blowup of Las Vegas. There was a box of Tootsie Rolls on the refrigerator and a case of Fritos on the floor and Buster Mano said take your pick. I tore open a bag of Fritos.

"Yes, sir, I know a lot of the folks at the Royal Polynesian," Buster Mano said.

I had the uneasy feeling that Buster Mano had done a make on me.

"What makes you think that?" he said.

"Instinct," I said.

"With that kind of instinct you should come in with me," he said.

"Then you did do a make?"

"Information is power." He said it without malice. He was a large bulky man with sad, quick eyes and, strangely out of context, small, immaculate hands, nails buffed, cuticles trimmed. They looked as if they had been transplanted onto the fatigued, graying mass of flesh that was the rest of him.

"You been here three weeks, you almost never go out," he said. "You're from L.A., you've got a wife, a kid, you got two cars, paid cash for one, paid off the other in three months, you rent your house, you pay your bills. And last Thursday night you brought a colored lady home to your apartment at three o'clock in the morning, she left at quarter to four."

"Jesus," I said. "Jesus Christ."

"The Lord's only Son," Buster Mano said. "That's what my wife would say."

"How'd you find all that out?"

"I called the Royal Polynesian and told them I was investigating some stolen credit cards in your name. You pay by Diner's, I got your Diner's number."

"Terrific."

Buster Mano shrugged. "I called a friend of mine in L.A., he called a friend of his in the credit bureau. Then I called back the Royal Polynesian and said you were clean."

"Thanks," I said. I wondered what ever had possessed me to call Buster Mano. I was in way over my head, this was not the Newman Club, this was not 1,000 condoms for the price of 750, this was the office of a constipated private eye convinced that information about unpaid bills and insignificant adultery constituted power. It was a chastising experience, being regarded as an insignificant adulterer.

"Listen," Buster Mano said, "everyone in Vegas knows what everyone else is doing." He seemed to want to reassure me. "So what."

"So nothing, I guess."

"You doing six?" Buster Mano said.

I must have looked bewildered.

"Doing six," Buster Mano repeated. "Six weeks' residence. For a divorce."

I shook my head.

"Then what are you in Vegas for? The climate?"

How does one explain a billboard that said, VISIT LAS VEGAS BEFORE YOUR NUMBERS UP.

Buster Mano began to unwrap a Tootsie Roll. "So why do you want to see me, then?"

It sounded fatuous to say that I had never met a private detective, that I had called him to kill time, to find out what he did and how he worked. I had found that out all too quickly.

Buster Mano pushed the Tootsie Roll into his mouth and farted pleasantly.

"Kid," he said—he could not have been more than ten years older than me, but I was still "Kid"— "you have come to the right place."

I wonder now why I did not just get up and leave the office. I can only suggest that I felt at home in this confessional of the meaninglessly illicit. The fact was also that I liked Buster Mano. He was a man without illusions. He expected the worst and the worst did not mean much. He viewed life, his own especially, as a hapless patchwork of small strategies and minor betrayals. There was a complicity between us that was missing in my relationship with Jackie Kasey. Buster knew what I was up to and it did not bother him; if I got something on him, that was all right, he had something on me, too. Tit for tat. We're both in the Peeping Tom racket, he liked to say, and he knew it made me uncomfortable.

The only release he sought was an unblocked colon. I shared with him an appreciation of functional humor and discourse. When I was a child my father, who was a surgeon, had operated on a boy to correct a stoppage of the rectum. The operation was successful and generated a stool of such dimension that it was pictured in the medical journals calibrated against a yardstick. Buster listened to this story as if it were homiletic. I also told him about a boy with whom I had grown up, Teddy Kentfield. When we were in the sixth grade, Teddy used to bottle his farts in an empty Alka Seltzer bottle. He would feel one coming on, uncap the bottle, screw it into his bum and let go. Teddy said that the secret in preserving the broken wind was in screwing the cap back on fast. He dated each bottle—February 9, say, to February 16—and kept each vintage on a shelf in his room. Sometimes he would sell a smell of a vintage of special bouquet, *un premier grand cru classe,* as it were, for a nickel a whiff. Buster smiled, Buster understood, Buster asked if that was how Teddy had financed his way through college.

•   •   •

A telephone call. Dorothy Terkel wanted Buster
to run a surveillance on her husband. Dorothy worked
in the cashier's office at the Mint. Her husband was a
pit boss at the Thunderbird. His name was Bob and he
had a girl friend in the administration office of the
Thunderbird. The girl friend's name was Mona. Dorothy wanted the surveillance so that she could file a
divorce action against Bob. Buster was perplexed.
"What Dorothy doesn't know is that Bob called me
yesterday and wants a surveillance on her," Buster said.
"Bob says she's fooling around with a guy named Phil
Fontaine who runs junkets into the Flamingo. It's an
ethical decision. Do I take Bob or Dorothy?"

Buster took neither.

Another telephone call. A downtown Las Vegas
law firm called Buster for references on Bob Farkas, a
local attorney seeking a new job with the firm. The
firm's senior partner had done business with Buster and
wished to know if he had ever worked with Bob Farkas
and if so what he thought of him. Buster allowed that
he knew Bob Farkas. He said that Bob Farkas drank a
lot, not enough to qualify as an alcoholic, but a lot. Bob
Farkas had never really made it on his own, no real
reason, he just never had. Perhaps it was the drinking,
perhaps it was his wife, a nice little girl named Carol.
Carol's problem was her ex-husband. The ex-husband
had been in the Air Force at Nellis, a jet jockey. He had
twice been passed over for major and there was talk
about a shortage in some officers' club funds that he was
handling. He was allowed to resign from the Air Force
and then he went to work for a flying circus, flying
professional sky divers. Then he worked as a crop

duster in the San Joaquin Valley. He was said to be a good pilot, but he changed jobs a lot. He was always on the move. Carol said she felt like a gypsy and finally divorced him. Bob Farkas had handled Carol's divorce and she had ultimately married him. He was older, settled, established, though not very successful. The trouble was that Carol's ex-husband, the captain, kept returning to Vegas between jobs, between the dusting seasons in the Imperial Valley and the San Joaquin Valley. He always stayed at the Marrakech Motel on Flamingo Road. He gambled, he took the sun, he saw old friends at Nellis, and afternoons at the Marrakech, he would entertain his ex-wife, Carol. Bob Farkas knew about the afternoons at the Marrakech, but did nothing and said nothing. He just drank a little more. The captain got married a couple more times and each time he got divorced, he got divorced in Vegas. And so every couple of years, Carol began to spend three or four afternoons a week at the Marrakech. They liked her ex-husband at the Marrakech. The help at the motel even called him "Captain," which he appreciated very much. When the girl at the desk got married, the captain gave her his old silver Air Force wings as a wedding present. It was things like that that made the captain so likable, and people said that this likability was the reason Carol came to see him those afternoons at the Marrakech between the crop-dusting seasons or whenever the captain was getting another divorce. Bob Farkas never met the captain, never knew how likable he was; he just kept on drinking a little more whenever the captain was in town. Then two years before, Carol had died of a stroke. An aneurysm near the brain that blew out like a tire. She was just twenty-nine. It happened at the Marrakech Motel. The captain called an ambulance, waited until the doctor arrived, then checked out of the motel. He had not been seen in Vegas since. Bob Farkas identified Carol's body at Southern Nevada Memorial Hospital. He could not help but notice that the captain had not done a very good job getting her dressed. He attended to all the funeral arrangements and had her ashes shipped to her only other relative, an aunt who lived in Elko.

Bob Farkas was still around, he was still available, he still drank a lot. Not enough to be classified as a lush, Buster Mano reassured the senior partner of the law firm, not enough to preclude hiring him. Buster Mano said that Bob Farkas would probably be good for research work, writing briefs and running down precedents, but Buster said he himself would not give him any trial work. The senior partner thanked Buster Mano for his time and trouble.

"That's why they call me," Buster Mano said when he hung up the phone. "I give it to them straight."

2

It was Buster Mano who told me the story about Artha, the prostitute, and Al Fogelson, the disappearing Kelvinator appliance salesman. He told it to me as an example of the kind of work that he did. But as it happened I had already met Artha on my own and was able to fill in a number of the blanks in his story.

I had met Artha because of my chronic insomnia. When I couldn't sleep and the late show was over, I would leave my apartment and wander through the casinos on the Strip. There is something restful about a casino at 5 A.M. The tourists have gone to bed, most of the tables have closed down and the slots are almost stilled. It is the time of the serious gamblers. There is no music from the showrooms, the hookers have mostly made their connections and there is only the soft rustle of money at the baccarat table and the serious hard-faced men for whom gambling seems an evangelical experience.

She was sitting in the keno lounge at the Flamingo. I remember that my immediate impression was of a corrupted nun. She was wearing a black pants suit with a white Peter Pan collar and an elaborate wig of sausage curls. She looked like one of those parochial-school girls I used to try to pick up when I was in my teens, Polish girls who took a business course in high school and worked in the factories of East Hartford and who were said to fuck. Night after night on my summer vacations, I would cruise the bars of déclassé East Hartford, an upper-middle-class adolescent with high-density acne and a fake draft card, sheltered by a carload of like-minded friends from the tonier suburbs to the west, all of us closet virgins convinced that the blue-collar proles loved it, they were different, they were hotter, they had silver tongues, these Polish girls, these Italian numbers, put an American flag over her face and fuck for Old Glory. We cruised and we blustered and night after night we drank rye and ginger ale and vomited in the back of the car and went home empty-handed, complaining hoarsely of lover's nuts, an affliction I am still not sure exists but which was an article of my post-pubescence.

That was why I was so struck by Artha the first

time I saw her in the keno lounge of the Flamingo. She was the memory of every ethnic that I had never, as we used to say, "got into." I could not take my eyes off her. I thought at first that she was playing keno, sitting there all alone at five in the morning, chewing on a black keno crayon, then bending over and writing feverishly on a keno ticket. She must have seen me staring at her, but she gave no indication.

Then she was paged by the hotel operator. "Miss Artha Ging, please, call for Miss Artha Ging."

She got up, fluffed her sausage curls and crumbled the keno ticket into an ashtray. I watched her go to a house telephone, talk briefly into it, then head for the baccarat table. The velvet rope was lifted and she took her place by one of those serious hard-faced men with a neat pile of hundred-dollar bills in front of him. He gathered his winnings, stuffed a hundred-dollar bill into the tuxedo pocket of the dealer, then taking Artha by the arm, walked across the casino to the elevator.

I thought, Well, someone was getting into an East Hartford girl. Finally.

I went back into the keno lounge and sat in the seat she had left. Desultorily I uncrumpled the keno ticket she had thrown into the ashtray. On the back of the ticket, in the same neat Palmer Penmanship hand that I had been taught by the Sisters of Mercy at Verbum Dei School in Hartford, was a verse:

> *Sometimes I find my life a*
> *   maze*
> *Of lonely nights and aspirin*
> *   days.*

Longing for the golden cup,
Terrified of waking up.
Easy eights and twenty-one,
A life that's over before it's
begun.

A poetry-writing hooker. I considered it. There, somewhere in the Flamingo Hotel, a poetess with sausage curls was banging a serious hard-faced man who had stuffed a hundred-dollar tip into the tuxedo pocket of a baccarat dealer. I read and reread the poem. I remembered a poetry course I had taken in prep school.

POETIC ANALYSIS

1. What is the meaning of the poem and what is experience? Moral? Physical? Mental?

2. What thought or reflection does the experience lead us to?

3. What *mood, feeling* or *emotion* is stirred by the poem *as a whole?*

4. What uses of the imagination are there in the poem? Are the word pictures vivid? striking? Are the words appropriate to the mood and the thought? Are

they simple common words or
are they colorful words?

CONDENSATION: The anagram TIRED

Thought
Imagination
Rhythm
Emotion
Diction

I somehow had never thought I would put these
Fourth Form lessons to use at 5 A.M. in the keno lounge
of the Flamingo Hotel on the Las Vegas Strip. (I
remember now something else I had written in that
poetry textbook: "*Canterbury Tales*—age-old story-
telling device—*Grand Hotel, Twentieth Century, Bridge
of San Luis Rey,* etc.")

> *Easy eights and twenty-one,*
> *A life that's over before it's*
> *begun.*

I was still giving the poem a close textual exege-
sis when I saw Artha come out of the elevator alone
about an hour later. She took a stool at one of the
service bars. Her poem in hand, I went over and sat
next to her. "Would you like a drink?"

"You following me around?"

There seemed no way out of it. "I guess I am."

"A shot of milk on the rocks, crème de cocoa
back," she told the bartender.

"That's a poet's drink," I said. My knack for the
pickup had not improved much since those nights in the
bars of East Hartford.

"You want to fuck or something?"

"Actually, no."

"You queer?"

"Actually, no."

"Actually or no?"

"No."

"You get your rocks off talking to hookers, is that it?"

It was a remark that hit perilously close to home. I had never subscribed to the youthful bravado that paying for it was slightly less satisfying than jerking off. I did like talking to hookers, I think out of some residual Catholic impression that as long as one did not handle the merchandise, one was committing only a venial and not a mortal sin.

"Actually, I read your poem," I said. I had the desperate sense that I was playing out a scene in a situation comedy.

"Yeah?" she said.

"Yeah."

"It's a piece of shit," she said.

"No, no, it's not."

She gargled her crème de cocoa, then quaffed it with some milk. "Yeah, then what's so good about it?" she said defensively.

I could almost hear the whirring of my memory drum: CONDENSATION: T-I-R-E-D. "It had thought, imagination, rhythm, emotion, diction."

She looked at me dubiously. "No shit?"

"No shit." We seemed to be fashioning a new style of teacher-student communication. "The word pictures were striking. Vivid."

"So how do you know so much?"

I said that I was a writer. It seemed an inadequate explanation, but it satisfied her. She snapped her fingers at the bartender. "Hit me again. A shot of milk on the rocks, crème de cocoa back."

I ordered an orange juice.

"You want to know what I just did?" she said.

"What you always do, I guess."

"No, this was a first for me." She seemed animated, enthusiastic. It was as if she had never considered the possibility that she might have talents other than fellatio. "This guy, big winner in baccarat, forty-seven hundred bucks, he wanted to suck my nose."

I had to let that sink in. "That's all?"

"Yeah, it was no big deal."

"Wait a minute," I said, "back up, take it from the top. He sucked your nose?"

She nodded.

"How?"

She was extraordinarily patient, as if explaining to a backward child. "We took off our clothes, got into bed, he climbed on top and honked my nose." She was the teacher now, the deviate's poetess. "Until he popped."

I did not comprehend, I could not begin to comprehend. "And that's all?"

"Yeah."

"Jesus."

"You think there's a poem in it?"

T-I-R-E-D. What thought or reflection does the experience lead us to?

We became friends, Artha and I. It was an odd, edgy friendship, at times hostile, the roles of teacher and student constantly switching between us. It took me a long time to realize that Artha was using me far

more than I her. Almost without knowing it, I became
a kind of surrogate pimp. I was the passport she needed
to cruise the casinos; as long as she was hanging on my
arm, she would never be busted by the vice. In payment
she gave me a glimpse of her life, and in the end these
glimpses were the same as the "free pussy" she gave to
the dealers and pit bosses who arranged her dates. She
was totally uninterested in my life, with the result that
I did not have to resort to the same subterfuges with her
that I did with Jackie. There was no question of treason;
it was strictly a business arrangement, and if we became
friends it was the way people who served together in the
army or who worked in the same office became friends.
Nothing personal.

    Ours was a celibate relationship, but even after
she was sure I was not just out for a free piece of ass,
she could turn ugly and mean. She regarded every man
as a potential trick and even in idle conversation communicated almost exclusively in the vocabulary of sexual encounter. Her most ready references were to blow
jobs and taking it in the ass and to men coming in her
hairpieces, and such was her emotional scar tissue that
she doled out each vignette as if it were an aphrodisiac,
some linguistic Spanish fly. I had the feeling that she
thought that the only way she could get anyone to listen
to her was through tall tales of sexual fantasy. She told
me once that the father of her child was the only man
she had ever fucked six times in one night, "plus a blow
job." It seemed the only way she could express her
feelings about him, as if his being able to fuck her six
times in one night somehow made him larger and better
than other men.

    She was Polish, her real name was Ginowski.
She came from Sheboygan and moved to Milwaukee

after her mother's second divorce. Her favorite teacher in high school made her read *The Reader's Digest* cover to cover every month, and she often thought that she could have "gone into journalism." In her last year in high school, when she was pregnant, she had joined the Book of the Month Club and was still a member. She had liked Michael Crichton's *The Andromeda Strain,* but thought Crichton's *Five Patients* was a "piece of shit, it should never have been a Book Club Selection." Her child was born when she was eighteen and immediately put out for adoption. She remembered that her room in the hospital was near the nursery.

I liked Artha. She was never the whore with a heart of gold and she would have had to cheat on an I.Q. test to get a score of 100. But she had a feral instinct for survival and I often had the feeling that the only reason she kept the statistics on her tricks was to prove her own worth, even in that left-handed form of human endeavor. Talking to her was like opening up a door into an unlighted basement. Often after seeing her I would walk alone through the casinos on the Strip, staring at all those men who looked like sun-tanned liver marks, all cardigan sweaters and pinky rings, men who seemed to have spent too much time in saunas and steam rooms and to have trafficked in too many stories about masseuses who went down on you, a little extra with the massage, and I would wonder who were the nose suckers and who were the nose suckees. If they sucked noses, I wondered what else was going on that I had never heard of, what baroque sexuality, wondered if there were special orifices drilled especially for the Vegas habitué, wondered what else was on tap.

PART

3

EIGHT

Iwas a virgin until four days before my twenty-first birthday. It was a source of some private shame. I never actually lied about my virginity. I just had the feeling that some arcane technical skill was involved, as in flying an airplane, and that if I were asked to prove my qualifications it would be like being asked to solo a P–38. So while I never claimed to be a "swordsman," the term then current at Princeton, I never admitted to being "cherry" either; I would just smile and nod a lot during the "Thank-God-they're-gone" bull sessions after a party weekend and grade my dates somewhere between six and nine on the sexual scoreboard.

"Did you make it?" I would be asked.

I would slam a fist into a palm. "Pow!"

It always seemed to suffice, I think, in retrospect, because so many others would give some variant of the "Pow!" and the fist in the palm. In fact I had only touched two pudenda in my life: the first, while in the seventh grade at Verbum Dei School, belonging to a twelve-year-old girl who later became a nun; the sec-

ond, while at Princeton, belonging to a girl from Centenary College, which I hardly thought remarkable, as
Centenary girls were generally regarded as socially in-
ferior and hence easy lays. (The accessibility of the
lower orders was an enduring myth of my youth, the
sexual equivalent of the Protocols of Zion. It was not
until I was in the Army—no longer a virgin—that I
became aware that the hash slingers and gas-station
attendants with whom I took basic training clung to the
equally enduring myth that the sexually constipated
girls with whom I had grown up were the real "mattress
backs," while their own sisters were in fact inviolate. It
is always "the Other" who populates our fantasies.)

I began to think of myself, in college, as a terminal virgin; masturbation became the morphine of my
life. I roomed alone my first two years and jerked off in
the morning when I woke up and then again before
dinner, generally while staring into the eyes of Terry
Moore, whom I had seen six times with Tyrone Power
in *King of the Khyber Rifles* and considered the most
ravishing creature since Botticelli's Venus. There had
been a colorchrome picture of her on the cover of the
New York *News*'s Sunday supplement and I had pinned
it to the back of my door, directly on the eyeline from
the pillow on my bed. Pouty of mouth, ample of cleav-
age, Terry on my door was a call to battle stations.

Freshman, sophomore, junior years—I never
came close to penetration. Friends would complain
loudly that their dates would only let them "dry
hump"; I began to think that if I were ever allowed the
opportunity to dry hump I would undergo a mystical
transformation. I did not think of myself as repressed.
It is an article of faith in some quarters that a Catholic

upbringing is by definition sexually repressive, but then they have never been exposed to the sex education available in a parochial schoolyard. On the playground of Verbum Dei School I learned in the third grade that girls had "three holes," though where the third was I had not the foggiest notion. In the fourth grade, Beef Hennessy came up with information from his sixth-grade brother, Lard (they were both big boys, the Hennessys), that one could ". . . eat pussy, it tastes a little like lamb." Still in short pants, I tried to visualize the scene: salt, pepper, knife, fork? My mental antennae could not tune in on the idea. And in the seventh grade, Eddie Toomey taught me how to masturbate.

"Ain't you ever whacked off?" he asked me incredulously one day at recess.

"They watch me like a hawk," I said.

"In the crapper?" Eddie Toomey said.

"No, they don't watch me in the crapper."

"Then what do you do in the crapper?"

"What do you usually do in the crapper?"

"Whack off."

It was a new concept of toilet training. "Oh."

"Ain't your brother ever taught you?" Eddie Toomey said.

My brothers were seven and eight years older than I and had neglected that part of my education. I mumbled something unintelligible.

"What kind of brother you got anyway?" Eddie Toomey said. "A fairy?"

"He's no fucking fairy." I wasn't sure what a fairy was, but it seemed a passable sibling defense.

Eddie Toomey bent low and demonstrated, fist pumping, thumb up. "Some guys wrap the thumb around it, too," he said. "I like to keep the thumb up."

Across the schoolyard I could see Sister Jericho watching us. My father had once operated on her and she had taken a special shine to me. Every Christmas there was a gift, some linen or a picture of the Immaculate Heart of Jesus.

"Sister's looking at us," I said.

"So what," Eddie Toomey said. "She's as blind as a fart."

"Yeah, but she's looking."

"What's she going to do," Eddie Toomey said, "tell Father Shea I was teaching you how to jerk off? How's a Sister supposed to know anything about pulling your pud?"

It seemed the quintessence of schoolyard wisdom. Eddie Toomey raised his fist, thumb up, and moved it up and down like a pendulum in the direction of Sister Jericho. I thought it the bravest thing I had ever seen.

"You got to keep the wrist loose," Eddie Toomey said. "Don't grip it too hard. Like you're playing ball. Like Bobby Doerr."

Bobby Doerr was the second baseman of the Boston Red Sox and I wondered if Eddie Toomey had ever watched him jerk off. At this point I would have believed him if he said he had seen the visions at Fatima.

"He's a wrist hitter," Eddie Toomey said. He snapped an imaginary bat at an imaginary ball. "I bet he really knows how to whack off."

That night, in the shower, I put Eddie Toomey's lessons to work. I bent low, kept my grip loose and my thumb up. The shower water cascaded over my shoulders. Nothing happened. I wondered if I was using the proper hand. I was right-handed, so naturally I was using that hand. Was I supposed to use the left? Was my wrist loose enough? I tried to envision Bobby Doerr at Fenway Park, snapping the bat, the ball disappearing over the Green Monster in left field.

And then, wonder of wonders.

Unfortunately Eddie Toomey had neglected to inform me about ejaculation. The pleasure was immediately compromised by the stream of liquid oozing down the cloth shower curtain. I furiously wiped at the pasty stain with soap and a washcloth. We had a maid then whom I had once seen on her day off in downtown Hartford wearing my mother's fur coat. She had sworn me to secrecy and so I knew I could count on her not to report the stain to my parents.

I wondered if she would know what it was.

The next day, in the schoolyard, Eddie Toomey said, "Did you shoot?"

Shoot—so that was what I had done. "Did I shoot?" I said. "You kidding? Is the Pope a Catholic?"

"Who'd you think of?" Eddie Toomey said. "Louisa Gambino?"

I had not realized that you were supposed to think of anyone.

Eddie Toomey was persistent. "Marie Cahill? She wears a brassiere. Sandra Sirota? Beef Hennessy says she's got hair."

I could not conjure up a name.

"You must have thought of somebody," Eddie Toomey said.

"Bobby Doerr," I said finally.

"You a fairy or something?" Eddie Toomey said.

From that moment on I would always think of

someone. June Haver. Joan Fontaine. Jeanne Crain. I
would think of Jeanne Crain and some celestial orchestra would strike up "Spring Fever." Restless as a willow
on a windstorm, jumpy as a puppet on a string. (I was
mortified years later when I discovered that the son of
one of these inspirations was in the same nursery school
as my daughter. "How do you do?" she said at the
Christmas pageant. I almost said, "We've met.") I also
began to have the fantasy that my pumping right hand,
thumb up, controlled the destiny of the Brooklyn
Dodgers. If I jerked off they would lose; French Bor-
dagaray would strike out with the bases loaded, Curt
Davis would walk home the winning run or Howie
Schultz would boot a double-play ground ball. The
Dodgers lost eighty-seven games in 1944 and finished in
seventh place. (In later years this fantasy took a different twist. If I balled whatever girl of the moment, the
Dodgers would win; in the tight pennant races of the
mid-fifties there were weeks when I would pray for rain
or an off day.)

I waited for the hair to grow on my palms and
measured myself every day to see if I had stopped growing. I found that smelling my sleeve or my pillow was
a powerful aphrodisiac. One sniff of the pillow and I
would be in the arms of Rhonda Fleming. My major
preoccupation was how to avoid soiling the bed linen.
I would breathe deeply of the pillow and then at the
moment of coming would race for the bathroom and
fertilize the toilet. It was my older brother who solved
the problem of staining the sheets. He was in the Army,
stationed in Mississippi, and was about to go to the
Pacific in preparation for the invasion of Japan. He
came home on leave and as a going-away present gave

me three packages of Sheik prophylactics. "So you won't have to change the sheets," he said.

I held the Sheiks in my hand. "Boy, that Mississippi must be some place."

"We get them free."

I nearly fainted. "At the PX?"

"Noooo." He was not yet twenty, had won a Bronze Star in Europe, and though only a private seemed to me the embodiment of the young officer in *Journey's End.* "You can't get a pass without showing your rubbers."

This was an Army that seemed to me bliss, much more to my liking than the trenches of *Journey's End.*

The summer I was sixteen I got my working papers and found a job with a wholesale drug company in downtown Hartford. Connecticut then had a prohibitive birth-control law and the sale of contraceptives was theoretically forbidden. Most drugstores, however, kept a supply of prophylactics in stock, ostensibly for medical prescriptions, but in fact sold them to whoever asked. The rubbers were kept in a refrigerated stockroom on the second floor. The first time I was sent to this stockroom I nearly became unhinged. Gross upon gross of Sheiks and Rameses and Trojans. Every day I volunteered to sweep out the stockroom and every day I would stuff my pockets with packages of rubbers. I stashed them in my closet at home, 196 packages, 588 rubbers in all, almost a year, I thought, of Nirvana.

Then my mother found them.

My father had died several years before, so she deputized my oldest brother—not the one who gave me the Sheiks—to talk it out with me. It was not a fruitful discussion.

"What did you intend to do with them?"

"Nothing."

"What do you mean, 'nothing'?"

"I mean, I was going to give them back."

"You stole them just so you could give them back?"

"I didn't 'steal' them, I 'took' them."

"Would you mind explaining the difference?"

Some of my bravado was returning by now. "I don't think *you* would understand."

I thought for a moment he was going to throw me across the room. He had played freshman football at Harvard and had a rather simple direct way of solving problems with his younger siblings. "Now, goddammit, why did you steal them?"

He knew why I had taken them as well as I did, but chronic masturbation seemed a concept he would just as soon avoid.

"Actually," I said, my brain beginning to work now, "I stole them for Austin Feeney."

I had gone to Verbum Dei School with Austin Feeney and he had always claimed that from the second grade on he had been "getting it regular." I had not seen him for years.

"Four gross for Austin Feeney," my brother exploded.

"He gets a lot."

2

The upshot was that I was sent away to boarding school. With my eldest brother getting married and
the next in college, it was decided in family council that
I very much needed male guidance. The consensus of
my elders was that I was sex-obsessed (I had taken to
calling one of my virgin sisters a "whooor," the pronun-
ciation favored in the circles in which I traveled) and
the hoarding of forty-nine dozen rubbers did little to
allay that suspicion. As I was too young for the Army
and not inclined to the seminary, boarding school
seemed just the ticket.

A Catholic school. Except for the occasional
wedding or christening or funeral, it is nearly twenty
years now since I voluntarily entered a church to help
celebrate the sacrament of the Mass, yet the Catholicism of my childhood remains the one salient fact of
my life. It was an experience predicated on habit rather
than on faith, a comforting habit, like a swim before
breakfast or a drink before dinner, so that when I
drifted away from the Church in later years it was less
a loss of faith than the erosion of a routine. If the
Church could not inculcate faith in its young penitent,
it could inculcate the habit of church-going. Confession
on Saturday, Mass and Communion on Sunday, the
Stations of the Cross on Wednesday. I loved confession,
the sense of a burden removed when one said the magic
formula, "Bless me, Father, I confess to Almighty God
and to you, Father, that I have sinned. It has been one
week since my last confession. These are my sins."
There had been the thorough examination of conscience beforehand, the registering of sins by command-

ment. It was all laid out in *The Child's Missal*:

EXAMINATION OF CONSCIENCE
1st Com: failure to pray, denial
or doubts of God?

2d Com: Cursing, swearing?

3d Com: Missing Mass
wilfully, irreverence in Church?

4th Com: Disobedience?

5th Com: Anger? Quarreling?

6th & 9th Com: Thoughts,
words or actions against
purity?

7th & 10th Com: Theft? Envy?
Discontent?

8th Com: Lying?

The object was to navigate the commandments
as one might a minefield, easing past the confessor a
convoy of mortal sins camouflaged as venial. Envy and
denying God were unimaginable; for Verbum Dei boys
between the ages of seven and ten, the sins that seemed
most to promise eternal damnation were shoplifting (I
was an incorrigible candy-bar thief during a brief reign
of dime-store terror in the second grade), lying and
swearing. In the pantheon of sins there were gradations

of swearing from "hell" to "damn" to "bitch" to "bastard" to "shit" to "fuck" to "God damn." No number of "fucks" could equal a single "God damn," because invoking the Almighty to condemn was intruding on God's work, the worst impertinence of all. In the painful years of puberty, swearing gave way to "lewd thoughts" in the confessional; "fuck" became less an obscenity than an ideal. And from the age of thirteen on, the sins of the flesh, each darting of the hand under the sheets in the dark of night.

"For these and all my other sins, I am heartily sorry and humbly ask pardon of God and penance and absolution from you, Father."

There was no subtle philosophical questioning of the right of the disembodied voice on the other side of the velvet-curtained screen to absolve. To question what a celibate knew about the desires of the dark was like wondering if a nun had breasts or pubic hair—the most mortal of sins. The main concern was wondering if Father Cleary had recognized your voice; did he or Father Fahey look strangely at you in the schoolyard? I knew of course about the secrets of the confessional, knew that no torture had yet been devised to make Fathers Fahey or Cleary reveal that I had violated the sixth and the ninth commandments, but nevertheless I alternately raised and lowered my voice every Saturday when I slipped into the confessional, a midget basso or a midget soprano depending on the week that was.

If I liked confession, I disliked Communion. The host tasted like a piece of old cardboard and tended to stick to the roof of the mouth. It was the most grievous offense to dig it out with your finger—the Consecration, after all, had turned the host from a

wafer into the body and blood of Our Lord Jesus Christ
—but with perfect piety, eyes closed, hands folded in
prayer in front of the face, one could slip a thumb into
the mouth and dislodge the glutinous dough. In fact I
tended to by-pass Communion. When the bells rang I
would leave my pew and head for the altar. But once
I gained the Communion rail I would lose myself in the
throng, sliding left or right along the altar until I was
beyond the vision of probing eyes, then when the priest
approached I would make a sharp U-turn, genuflect
elaborately and return to my seat, the very picture of
the sanctified communicant.

I found the pageantry of the Mass terribly reas-
suring. It was something no other religion had. There
was that moment at a Catholic funeral when the priest
in his purple chasuble approached the casket and
anointed it with incense. At that instant, I would always have the sense, as I have never had at the funeral
service of any other denomination, that a life had been
lived and a man had died and that no matter how paltry
the life or insignificant the man, it was important
enough to merit this heliotrope production number.

"*Misereatur vestri omnipotens Deus,*" the priest
would intone, "*et dimissis peccatis vestris, perducat vos
ad vitam aeternam.*"

"Amen," I would whisper, and the tears would
start. I always cried at Catholic funerals.

But ultimately church-going became like watching too many Rose Parades; year after year the same
petaled floats, tea roses and floribunda and grandiflora
and climbers and polyantha and perpetuals and dam-
asks and moss roses and French roses and cabbage
roses and musk roses and albas and Bourbons and Noi-

settes and China roses and sweetbriers and shrub roses
and tree roses, millions and millions of petals of every
variety and every hybrid and every color, but finally,
just roses. One remembered the Rose Parade fondly,
but with no real desire to go back next year. In this
twilight of habit, the sliding Catholic was left only with
belief, and there was the rub. We Catholics were supposed to believe; we were good at it. How else could
Mother Church be like Mother Courage, a survivor
since 33 A.D.? Each succeeding generation tried to ex-
cise doubt for the sake of the next. Murder, adultery—
they could be absolved in the confessional. But apostasy
condemned the heretic to a life without joy or laughter
or spiritual sustenance. Apostates were not invited to
dinner. I remember once seeing a backslid friend of the
family at a Yale-Dartmouth game. He was with one of
those blond Peck & Peck girls in a polo coat and they
laughed and hugged and kissed with every succeeding
Dartmouth score and I wondered why he was not more
burdened, how he could be so carefree without receiving the Sacraments. I was eleven that year.

The Church triumphant, the Church militant,
the Paraclete, the litany of the saints—they were to be
invoked during those recurring crises of faith. There
was a theological meanness about the Church that
nagged. Partial and plenary indulgences were doled out
like trading stamps, a hoard against bad time in purgatory; children mouthed their aspirations and filled their
mite boxes as if they were making time payments on a
special-fare ticket to the Big Vacation in the Sky. Education in a parochial school had a certain teleological
bent. I learned more about Father Isaac Jogues and the
other French missionaries along the Mississippi than I

did about Roger Williams in Rhode Island, the Puri-
tans in the Massachusetts Bay Colony or Wolfe and
Montcalm on the Plains of Abraham. The nuns thought
the beleaguered Maryknoll missionaries in far-off pagan
China more central to its history than the Boxer Rebel-
lion; the rise of Mao Tse-tung could be laid to empty
mite boxes. It was an embattled view of history with
some strange villains (those awful Huguenots, for example) and even stranger heroes (the papal inquisitors
and the Bourbon monarchs), yet there was a sense of
martial identification with those tattered ensigns of cru-
sades past.

 I said apostates were not invited to dinner; nor
were Protestants. Jews were confined to an area of the
city that the arriviste Irish called "Kikes' Peak"; the
colored cleaned. This self-enclosed cloister led to a most
uncatholic view of the world, but perhaps that was the
point. Not much currency was lent to the idea that to
defend one's faith was to strengthen it. Within the fortress there were certain social dogmas at least as unas-
sailable as the Ten Commandments. First and foremost
there was the matter of "having a vocation." The
propaganda began almost with birth. Nothing was
more to be desired than the son who entered the priest-
hood, nothing could more increase the value of a family's social shares on the Catholic stock market. For the
parent the priest-son was the ultimate plenary indul-
gence; one basked in the reflected glory of a vocation.
I knew mothers who called their clergyman sons "Father," or, if especially intimate, "Father Jim." Through
the mists of time I have the sense of sons hustling into
the seminary with the same fervor that led others after
Pearl Harbor to enlist in the Marine Corps. Once in-

side, it was unacceptable to go A.W.O.L.

For daughters a vocation was a slightly different matter; the convent was a way to by-pass the stigma of spinsterhood. A spinster sister, we used to say in the schoolyard, is as useless as tits on a nun. Daughters existed to marry and reproduce. A woman with ten children was more worthy than one with two. The existence of only two children was usually explained as the result of a tipped uterus; when fueled with drink, the explanation was "Vatican roulette." Though rhythm was permitted by the Church, there were those who still regarded it as an exercise in promiscuity; better to die in childbirth than offend the Lord. And if there was a crisis in childbirth, if there was a choice between the mother's life or the child's, the Church opted for the new soul. I remember once asking my father, who was a surgeon, what he would do if confronted with such an emergency. "It never happens," he said. "It's never that clear-cut."

What breached this fortress, what let in the winds of secularism, was the reality of upward mobility. The lucky Irish went from steerage to suburbia in three generations. My maternal grandfather arrived in this country a few years after the Civil War, an unlettered child of twelve out from belowdecks and the ould sod, a placard around his neck on which was scrawled his name to identify him to his American relatives. He died seventy years later, rich and revered, as the *Luftwaffe* was blitzing London. He was a grocer who prospered and founded a bank. When I was born he was deep in his seventies, given to poetry and aphorisms, "If wishes were horses, beggars would ride." He favored charity and hated welfare. Thanksgiving and Christmas, there

were turkeys for the poor and presents for their children. One of his daughters married my father, a doctor
out of Catholic University and Harvard Medical
School. I was the fifth child of six and my brothers and
sisters and I were Harvard, Yale, Princeton, Williams,
Republican, Cotillion, Junior League and Bachelors'
Club.
    Once exposed to the larger world, faith collapsed
like a soufflé. Not that what replaced it was any better.
There were years of my youth when I was slightly
ashamed of my origins. I would scant the Catholic
University years of my father's education and tell my
Protestant friends that he had gone to Harvard. I wondered why my grandfather, nearing eighty and the chairman of his bank, would still go to his grocery store every
day, why he had to put on a white coat and a straw
boater and dispense sweets from the cookie barrel and
supervise the butchering of meat. I wondered why our
maids were not the faithful black retainers my friends
had, why they had to come from the House of the Good
Shepherd, fallen Catholic girls with checkered sexual
backgrounds and hair under their arms. (My brother
and I once put a wad of bubble gum in the armpit of a
sleeping Portuguese girl who worked for us, trying to
induce her to shave her armpits.) I was patronizing to
the Irish a generation behind me on the social ladder,
those who avidly perused the society pages to see if any
Catholics had made the Junior League or the Bachelors'.
I lost my faith and I lost my Irish and it was years later
before I realized that I was the poorer for it.

3

Portsmouth Priory, where I was sent after the episode with the rubbers, was a school in Rhode Island run by Benedictine monks. Its major claim to fame in 1948 was the erroneous rumor that it was the school where Bing Crosby had sent those four problem sons who later married (over and over) Vegas chorines. I never knew the source of this rumor, and the monks wearied of denying it, but whenever in later years I mentioned going to Portsmouth, the information was greeted with elaborate eye-rolling and palm-shaking and the assertion, "Oh, yeah, Gary Crosby went there," or Lindsay or Dennis or Phil. I once saw one of the baby Crosbys in Vegas with his show girl of the moment and was tempted to ask him where in fact he had gone to school, but he was on his way to get married and I never got the chance.

A number of the monks at Portsmouth were converts to Catholicism and all of them seemed engaged in a constant struggle to retain their faith. That priests could entertain doubt or consider despair was an entirely new, and invigorating, idea to me. That the Bible was not to be interpreted literally and that evolution precluded the actuality of Adam and Eve were heady concepts to one previously only exposed to religious who were inclined to answer queries about Darwin with a liberal application of the rubber hose syncopated to the question, "Do you still believe your grandfather was a monkey?" The monks swore and were not unappreciative of the older sisters and younger mothers who visited on weekends and sometimes would confide that the worst part of monastic life was being cloistered with a number of men they could not stand. Constantly wrestling with the larger problems of faith, they were far more tolerant in the confessional of the small sexual vices of their charges. Before going to Portsmouth, I would confess to a secular priest, "I had impure thoughts nine times"—ninety times nine was more like it—"and committed impure actions eleven times."

"With yourself or someone else?"

The shame of it. "Myself."

"A dozen rosaries. *Absolvo te* . . ."

It took approximately as long to say a dozen rosaries as it would to climb Golgotha on one's knees. In the confessionals of Portsmouth, penance for the same recital of sexual fantasy recognized the fallibility of the confessor as much as that of the penitent. "One Our Father, one Hail Mary and . . ." A long silence.

"Yes, Father?"

"Pray for me . . . if you can remember."

The founder of Portsmouth Priory had been an Episcopal priest before his conversion to Catholicism. He was, in 1948, in the last year of his life, over eighty, deaf and halt, but he would still try to maintain his priestly duties, saying Mass and occasionally hearing confession. The old boys at the school would indulge themselves in a peculiar kind of torture of the new students, a hazing involving old Father Hugh.

"Go to confession to Father Hugh," they would tell the unsuspecting new boy. "He's a cinch. You can tell him you banged your sister and all you'll get is a Glory Be."

The new boy would enter Father Hugh's confessional. It was a signal for a coven of old boys to huddle outside the box and listen, trying to stifle their laughter.

"Bless me, Father, for I have sinned . . ."

"WHAT'S THAT, LAD?" Father Hugh's voice would thunder from the confessional. He was by then so deaf that he had to shout to hear the sound of his own words. "MASTURBATION, IS THAT WHAT YOU SAID?"

A strangled whisper from the penitent.

"HOW MANY TIMES?"

Another whisper.

"SAME AS LAST WEEK, EH? NO MORE. WELL, THAT'S AN IMPROVEMENT. YOU'RE A GOOD LAD."

Their shame was so intense that some of the younger boys would actually refuse to come out of the confessional. Others would emerge in tears. No one ever confessed to Father Hugh more than once.

It was at Portsmouth that I first learned about the Coker sisters, Phyl and Norma. The Cokers were dime-a-dance hostesses at the Lido on Times Square in New York and a number of the older boys from New York claimed not only to have gone to the "Big L," as it was called, but actually to have laid either Phyl or Norma, if not both. The New York boys were far more sophisticated than the rest of us from the provinces. They went to the Stork Club and to La Rue and to debutante parties during Christmas vacation. And unlike those of us from places like Hartford and Detroit and Providence, they owned their own dinner jackets instead of renting them.

"Where you from?" one of the New Yorkers asked, my first day at Portsmouth.

"Hartford," I replied.

"I think I've heard of it."

It seemed the ultimate in chic. All the New

Yorkers talked about going "to the country" for the
weekend, by which, of course, they meant the Hamp-
tons, but I appropriated the term for myself. I never
went home to Hartford for the weekend without passing out the information that I was off to "the country."

Desperate to lay siege to the "Big L," I schemed
for the privilege of spending a weekend in New York.
My opportunity came on an honors weekend. I dressed
carefully—maroon school blazer with the Portsmouth
crest on the breast pocket; it seemed to an acned six-
teen-year-old with a painful stammer the perfect attire
to impress Phyl and Norma Coker. The Lido was on the
second floor and all the way up the stairs I could feel
the tightening in my groin. I was too nervous to be
disillusioned by the framed photographs of the dance-
hall hostesses lining the stairwell, each a study in the
ravages of the flesh. Palms wet with sweat, I bought a
dollar's worth of tickets, lit a cigarette and tried to act
casual. Though it was three years after Hiroshima and
seven since Pearl Harbor, the only song on the jukebox
seemed to be "Praise the Lord and Pass the Ammuni-
tion." A girl came around the railing, snatched the
tickets from my hand, ground her crotch clockwise into
my tumescence, repeated the motion counterclockwise
and then said my time was up. I had been on the floor
less than two minutes.

"Cute coat," the girl said, tracing the school
crest.

"Actually I'm from Portsmouth Priory."

"You cherry?"

"It's a Benedictine school in Rhode Island."

"Got any money?"

"The monks are really good guys."

"Give me twenty and I'll meet you later."

"Dollars?"

"No, cents."

"Say, you wouldn't happen to be Phyl Coker, would you?"

"She's having her period."

"That's interesting."

"Why?"

"Like a cigarette?" All things considered, I thought I was handling myself well.

"You come?"

Actually I had.

4

In the fall of 1950 I went to Princeton, having, it seemed, majored in the Big L during the remainder of my stay at Portsmouth, albeit without losing my virginity. On my application for admission, there was a question that asked, "Why do you wish to attend Princeton?" I puzzled over the answer for days before writing, "To make contacts for later life." In retrospect it does not seem the answer likely to have been made by Adlai E. Stevenson, Class of '23, or Francis Scott Key Fitzgerald, Class of '18. It was an answer more fitting to a future regional sales manager of the Scott Paper Corporation, and perhaps explains why I was so uncomfortable during my four years at Princeton. Throughout my tenure I was never really anything more than an adjunct of my roommate, who was subsequently voted "Most Likely To Succeed" in my class. It was by hanging onto his shirttails that I managed to

be invited to join an eating club. I remember the final
night of rushing, or "bicker," as it was called at Princeton. I had already been told that I was going to be bid
to join the club at the specific request of my roommate,
and at seven-thirty in the evening, I entered the front
door and was quickly ushered into an upstairs sitting
room. There I was informed that while indeed the invi-
tation was still open it would perhaps be best if I did
not sign the bicker book until nine or nine-thirty. The
explanation was that it would be an inducement to a
large group of undecided big men on campus to join the
club if other, more prominent names in the class appeared in the bicker book before mine. I was told not
to take it personally, and it was a measure of my in-
security that I didn't.

In four years I failed to make any mark at all at
Princeton. In my Senior Class Poll I was overlooked in
such categories as "Most Versatile" or "Most Original"
or "Done Most for Princeton." In fact my only showing
was a smattering of votes for "Summa Cum Lunch-
eon," a Princeton Latinate euphemism for "out to
lunch." We were quintessentially Silent Generation, my
classmates and I; the ultimate reward was a vice-presi-
dency of Proctor & Gamble. It was an attitude that ill
prepared us for the sixties. Years later, reading the class
notes in the *Alumni Weekly* or the biographical sketches
especially compiled for our tenth-reunion classbook
was like trying to crack a code. It was a time of emotional retrenchment, the hemorrhaging of ambition; the
once-perfect little wives named Mimsy and Pookie were
drifting into alcoholism and adultery. Mine was not a
class of would-be artists, composers and writers; the
Class of 1954 subscribed to the business ethic, and now

the man who would corner corn was perplexed to find himself in wholesale hardware in Harrisburg. "After I failed my foreign service exams," began the sketch of one of my classmates, as an undergraduate a young man whose life seemed etched with promise. Another gave only his address: "Room 30, Y.M.C.A., Ninth and Spring Streets, Warren, Pennsylvania." And another: "The uneventful has become eventful and we have become accustomed to it."

In fact the only thing I remember with any clarity of my four years at Princeton was the unrelenting pursuit of a sexual education. The Coker sisters were as famous at Princeton as they were at Portsmouth Priory. Two seniors in Colonial Inn had even invited them to house parties the spring of my freshman year, and they had responded to the rigors of an Ivy League weekend with a lofty aplomb that won them admiration up and down Prospect Street. Though both their dates passed out and disappeared from the fray early in the weekend, the Cokers refused all professional entreaties with the airy reply that this was a social and not a business weekend, an outing, as it were, in the country. Perhaps they were merely fatigued; a year later I was a bartender during reunion week and fell into conversation with a drunken member of the Class of '35, who asked if I had ever known Phyl and Norma Coker. I assured him that I had, in every possible way.

"Phyl Coker was my first piece of ass," he said.

I had a sinking feeling. "When was that?"

"Fall of freshman year."

The fall of his freshman year was 1931. Hoover was president, Franklin Roosevelt was in Albany, Hin-

denburg and the Weimar Republic were still afloat, the
dollar was not, and I had not even been born. But then
I rationalized: If Phyl were seventeen in that fall of 1931
when the St. Louis Cardinals beat the Philadelphia A's
in the World Series, as Pepper Martin, the Wild Horse
of the Osage, ran wild, then she would in that spring of
1952 be in the full bloom of womanhood. (It is a source
of wonderment to me now that Phyl Coker, then
twenty-one years in the prostitution game, could have
become in my mind a kind of Infanta to whom I had
been pledged, if not from birth, at least from near puberty. From the moment I first heard her name in the
monastic corridors of Portsmouth Priory I knew that I
would lose it to her and only to her. It was like the
mating of a sickly younger son of some obscure royal
house to the ripe and fertile princess of a minor Balkan
principality.)

Four days short of my majority, in an effort to
preserve my sanity, I finally made contact with Phyl
Coker. It was two thirty on a Wednesday afternoon, I
had twenty-five dollars in my pocket and a cherry to be
plucked. I called from a bar on 42nd Street. My throat
was dry. "I'd like to speak to Phyl Coker, please."

"This is Phyl, dear." The voice was sultry, in-
sinuating, more worldly than Terry Moore's in *King of
the Khyber Rifles.*

"Phyl, I'm a good friend of George Bainbridge's . . ." This was the form: mention a steady
client. I felt as if I were applying for guest privileges at
Piping Rock.

"George who, dear?"

"Bainbridge."

"I don't think I know anyone by that name,

dear." I thought with sinking heart that there had been a coup in the principality; the republicans had taken over. Then after a moment, she said, "Yale?"

Relief. "Princeton."

"A big boy. He plays football."

"Jayvee."

"J.V. who, dear."

"I meant junior varsity. George. He doesn't suit up for the games. Except when someone's hurt. Like in the Rutgers game last fall. He didn't play. He won't get his letter. I don't think."

"I see, dear." Silence. "Is there anything you want, dear?"

"Well, I just happened to be in town and I was wondering if I might pop by for a while."

"You play ball, dear?"

"No, actually."

"That's nice. Boys who play ball tend to be too big, don't you think?"

"It's certainly the case in football. Basketball, too. You actually don't have to be that big to play baseball, though."

"I see." Another silence. "You have a little present for Phyl, dear?"

"George mentioned twenty."

"Who?"

"George Bainbridge."

"The jayvee."

Her apartment was on East 52nd Street, a walk-up. The flat was on the top floor. I rang the bell and climbed the stairs. My feet were like concrete and there was not a drop of saliva in my mouth. Phyl was waiting on the landing. The Infanta looked like Anne of Cleves.

She had a square stocky figure and a face like a gravel pit. I was ready to turn around and race back downstairs. She made virginity seem viable.

"Hello, dear, what's your name?" She was wearing a cheap, thin negligee.

"Philip." Philip the Insecure. It was as if by giving an alias I would be preserving a section of virtue in the emotional north forty. Already I had taken all identification from my wallet and thirty extra dollars and put them in a locker at Grand Central. The key was stuck under the tray of a telephone booth at Grand Central with a wad of gum. There was nothing to rob and if I died, like John Garfield, in the saddle, I would be unidentifiable and hence not a source of shame to family in Hartford. Like Judge Crater, I would simply vanish from the landscape.

We went inside the apartment. It was a nondescript affair of Salvation Army chairs and couches. The only distinctive touch was the banners on the wall. Football banners from every school in the East—Princeton, Harvard, Cornell, Brown, Williams, Amherst, Dartmouth, Columbia. And then there were varsity letters and beer mugs and a monogrammed chair from the Harvard Coop and photographs of the Whiffenpoofs and the Nassoons. It was like being at a table down at Mory's. In that one room there was a history of the Ivy League from the days of the Bonus March on Washington to the McCarthy-Army hearings.

"You notice anything, dear?" Phyl said.

"It's very unusual."

"Nothing from the state universities," Phyl said. "I don't like the boys from the state schools. They're really not gentlemen."

I did some rapid figuring. There were approximately thirty thousand students in the Ivy League. It seemed enough for Phyl to handle without bothering with the vulgate from the state universities.

Phyl purred, "Norma, come out and meet my friend Philip. He's from Princeton."

Norma Coker materialized from another room. Like her sister, Norma was wearing a cheap negligee. They looked enough alike to be twins. "Oh, he's nice, Phyl."

"You think so, Norm?"

"I bet he's got a big one, Phyl."

"I guess you're kind of envious, Norm."

"Next time," Norma said to me, "you call Norm."

Phyl's hand found its way inside my pants. I tried to think cool thoughts. I was convinced that both Phyl and Norma knew it was my first time.

Norma began to rummage through a drawer and finally pulled out some photographs. "I think you'll like these," Norma Coker said. It was a grainy, out-of-focus photo of a couple in an advanced stage of cunnilingus. "It's Tom Neal and Barbara Payton."

Barbara Payton was an actress who had been married to Franchot Tone. Their marriage was a volatile affair that had made all the tabloids when she left him for a quasi-actor named Tom Neal.

"You can tell Tom by his tattoo," Norma said.

"You're going to get Philip all hot, Norm," Phyl said.

"Oh, would I love to be in your place, Phyl."

There was a tiny sway-backed bed in Phyl's room and over it a square blue and white banner that said, "For God, For Country And For Yale." Phyl took off her negligee. Her body was shaped like a fire hydrant and she had shaved off her pubic hair. "Don't worry about getting me pregnant," Phyl said. The thought had never crossed my mind.

"Ooooo."

"Ahhhh."

From the other room came the sound of Norma's voice. "How's it going, Phyl?"

"Ohhhh, Norm."

"Philip, I am so jealous," Norma said. And then: "I'm making some lemonade, you both want some? It's just the thing to cool you off when you're hot."

"I am so hot, Norm," Phyl said.

The telephone rang. I could hear Norma pick it up in the other room. "Alan, I don't know any Alans, you're going to have to refresh my memory, where you from, Alan?" Norma said. "Franklin and Marshall?" A pause. "Phyl," Norma shouted, "do we know anyone from Franklin and Marshall?"

Phyl was too busy to answer.

"Well, who else do you know, Alan?"

I wanted to shout, "Alan, for Christ's sake, tell her you're a friend of George Bainbridge's."

"You play football, Alan?" Norma said. Another pause. "Why don't you come by, then. You have a little present for Norm? That's nice, Alan. You like lemonade? It's just the thing to cool you off when you're hot."

5

I ultimately gave Norma a chance to turn a profit on her envy and then Phyl said *she* was jealous and then I was out of Princeton and into the Army and I did not see them for the rest of the fifties and most of the sixties, seventeen years in all, and I left New York and moved to California and my shoulders began to soften. I felt like an engine in need of an overhaul, and then one afternoon when I was briefly back in New York, a couple of wars and a few assassinations after that first coupling under "For God, For Country And For Yale," I called Phyl Coker to find where the years had gone and what they had meant and it was she who said, "But Jesus, darling, I'm sixty-two years old."

PART

4

NINE

The almanac in the morning paper said it was the 228th day of the year, the moon was between its last quarter and a new phase, the morning stars were Venus and Saturn, the evening stars were Mercury, Mars and Jupiter, it was the birth date of Robert Ringling and the anniversary of Babe Ruth's death and on that date in history gold had been discovered in the Klondike, Dwight Eisenhower had suffered his seventh heart attack and an air crash in Lake Michigan had claimed all thirty lives aboard.

There were two other items of note. A whorehouse in Storey County, eight miles east of Reno, had refused to cater to black customers. Federal officials were considering a complaint that the prohibition constituted a violation of the Public Accommodations Section of the 1964 Civil Rights Act.

The second item noted that there would be an underground nuclear test the following morning at the Atomic Energy Commission's Nevada test site at Mercury, sixty-five miles north of Las Vegas. I had been in Nevada long enough to know that the best way to experience a test was to stay up the night. The device (it was never called a bomb) was usually detonated in the moments before dawn and the mind played tricks. Was there a tremor? Did the lights dim as they do near a prison the night of an electrocution? One stays awake to feel a slight shiver of history and invariably there is the same sullen disappointment that one experiences watching an eclipse of the moon or another astronaut gamboling across the Sea of Tranquility. The instinct of the reporter takes over and with it the malignant knowledge that disaster is good copy. It is not something that one wishes to happen. It is simply a contingency not to be overlooked, a fact of the profession, as death is to the pathologist. Will there be a seepage of nuclear particles? What are the wind currents? How will Vegas react? Are those jaunty little men with the umber toupees the stuff of heroes? Can they mobilize themselves from the baccarat tables and the fellatio beds to save a city? Forget the cosmic question of whether Vegas deserves to be saved. Remember the astronauts. Were they who had made the moon seem less an adventure than a parlay ever so human as when the alarm bells rang in space?

The moment passes. It is all anticlimactic. The twitching of the earth might only be a clap of thunder. That afternoon, vaguely disappointed at not being vaporized, I took some steam at the Riviera. The other two men in the steam room seemed oblivious to my presence.

"You ever been in the slam?"

"No." Steam, sweat. "You ever been in the slam?"

"Yeah, I've been in the slam."

A long pause. "Now that I think of it, I been in the slammer, too."

2

Jackie Kasey picked up the house phone in the lobby of the hotel. "Hi, hon, it's Brother JayJay. Would you page Miss Kitty Litter for me, please?" He listened for a moment to the objections of the hotel operator. "Hon, would I kid you? She has a group. Kitty Litter and the Kats. They play the lounge at the Riv." He listened again. "What do you mean, I'm always putting you on. Dis is Brudda JayJay. Honest, hon, just page her for me."

It was hot, 107° outside, and there was nothing to do but wander the lobby, checking the action at the tables, seeing what conventions were in town. Yamaha was due in, 1,250 Yamaha dealers, and that was good, car dealers and motorcycle dealers, they drank a lot, they played a lot, they fucked a lot, they made everybody in Vegas happy. Better 1,250 Yamaha dealers than 40,000 Lions. The Lions had been in earlier in the summer and it was orange-juice punch spiked with lemon sherbet. The only thing the Lions forgot to do was spend. It was the biggest convention in the history of Vegas and all the Lions did was watch, they were very good watchers. They watched outside the curtains at the lounges, but did not go in, they did not have to, they could hear what the acts onstage were doing and they were not stuck with the two-drink minimum. They did not drink, the Lions, except for soda, which they called pop, and they did not gamble and they did not eat much except for hamburgers and pancakes and steak and eggs, the coffee shops made a killing out of the Lions, but the hotels in Vegas don't make a go on their coffee shops and the hotels were glad to see the last of the 40,000 Lions, they felt more at home with people like motorcycle dealers, the Yamaha boys, they've got peckers, show me someone with a pecker and I'll show you someone who's going to have a good time, the trouble with the Lions is they don't have no peckers.

The hotel operator paged, "Miss K. Litter, please, Miss K. Litter."

"The cunt's got no class," Jackie Kasey said.

It was his day off, it was too hot to drive across the desert back to Los Angeles and nothing to do then but turn around and toodle on back to Vegas. It was like being on an aircraft carrier, playing Vegas, for days on end not leaving the hotel, everything was there, food, drink, fun, a little head, nothing to do outside in the daytime but watch people get heatstroke. Like the guy in the newspaper that morning, a paraplegic, he had gone out into the desert so he could meditate for a while in solitude, he just wanted to get away. He had brought along a tent, an adequate supply of food and water, a rifle and a wheelchair, but something had gone wrong, the tent was never set up, the wheelchair had thrown a wheel and the paraplegic had baked to death, "literally baked to death," said the deputy sheriff who had identified the paraplegic outside Coyote Springs, near a whorehouse named Sherri's, where a customer could have a forty-dollar party, which included two girls, a porno movie and a dog, and could put the whole tab on his Master Charge card.

Jackie Kasey picked up the house phone again. He was taping a local television show in an hour, there was time to kill, he would goose the hotel operator again, it was a good *schtick*.

"Hi, hon, it's Brother JayJay again. Would you page Mike Hunt for me, please, hon. Mike Hunt."

Jackie Kasey hung up the phone, he was pleased, he had got her this time.

"Call for Mr. Mike Hunt, please," the hotel operator paged. "Mike Hunt."

"Say it slow," Jackie Kasey said to me.

"Mike Hunt," I said.

"Mike Hunt. My cunt. Get it." He slapped his hands, did a little dance and lapsed into baby talk. "I'm going to tell the assistant manager, I'm going to tell the assistant manager, one of the operators is saying dirty words, one of the operators is saying dirty words."

Jackie felt better. There was nothing like putting on a hotel operator to get the day off to a good start. Even his cold felt better, it always felt better in the daytime. Last night his cold had been bad. One of the reasons that his cold had been bad last night was that he had spent the evening with some agents from the William Morris office. He had not wanted to spend the evening with the Morris agents, it had just turned out that way. The Morris agents were in Vegas checking out some of their variety clients and they had run into Jackie and they had said "Hi," and he had said, "Hi," and no one knew quite what to do after that. Jackie had once been a client of the Morris office and they used to send him letters and the letters would say, "The entertainment world is going to enrich you spiritually and financially and we at the William Morris office are gratified to know that we will be of constant assistance in this ongoing process"; and the letters would say, "You are still stretching and you have not yet reached the giant height you will reach in this business"; and the letters would say, "I have seen Jolie (the late Al Jolson) and Frank and Dean and Jerry and at this comparable stage in your career you are matching them in knowledge of your craft, that is the craft of entertainer, entertainer of those people whose lives need your kind of light"; and the letters would say, "The entertainment industry has its General Motors and its General Electric and so sure are we that you are going to be a General Jackie that the U.S. Mint is not coining enough silver for us to give up being your agents while you ride the freeway to fame"; and the letters would say, "Not only would we stick out our neck for you, we would stick out our shoulders, arms and waist for you, and if your good wife Roxy will excuse a little harmless profanity, we would even stick out our *tush* for you." And the letters would sign off, "Affectionately, Your Friends & Representatives . . ."

There had been a parting of the ways between Jackie and his friends and representatives; the giant height had never been reached, the necks were no longer stuck out. The night before, Jackie had gone to Bill Cosby's opening in the big room at the International. Cosby had seen Jackie in the lobby and told him to come to the opening, he would introduce him from the stage, Ladies and gentlemen, a true star, my very good personal friend, Jackie Kasey. Jackie had not wanted to go to Cosby's opening, his cold was not good, but Cosby was a superstar, Leslie Uggams warmed up for him and Leslie Uggams was a headliner at the Riviera in her own right, and the true superstars brought out all the big agents and Strip bookers to their opening nights, so it was best to attend, especially if Bill Cosby had promised to introduce his very close personal friend from the stage. It was the kind of introduction that might help a semi-name become a name and that was something to consider. Jackie dressed carefully for

Cosby's opening dinner show, a brown double-knit suit with flared pants and matching tie, shirt and handkerchief. The effect was a little like an optical illusion, but at least when Cosby introduced him from the stage nobody in the audience could say he had missed him, he's the little guy in the optical-illusion brown in the banquette down front and center. Everything was set, the management comped the check, Jackie toyed with his roast prime rib of beef au jus garni, Cosby came out, did fifty minutes on Fat Albert and Weird Harold and forgot to introduce his close personal friend, Jackie Kasey. Jackie just sat on the banquette watching the cherries jubilee melt, occasionally stirring them around in the dish with his spoon, like a child playing with toy boats in a bathtub.

After the show Jackie went out into the lobby and there were the William Morris agents, who were now Cosby's friends and representatives, and Jackie said "Hi" and the Morris agents said "Hi" and they stood around smelling each other's toilet water.

"You like this toilet water?" Barry Stern said. He was cue-bald and was wearing a double-knit blue blazer with gold buttons and a Monagesque crest. "My barber gets it in Paris."

"He gets it from Paris," Mel Stavitz said. "Is that right?"

"He gets it *in* Paris," Barry Stern said. There was an element of pique in his voice, as if it had been suggested that his barber ordered eau de cologne from a toilet-water jobber like any simple merchant. "He goes a couple of times a year. More than that if someone's doing a picture there. He'll fly over for the weekend to do a trim."

"I've never been to a good barber in Paris."

"Nobody as good as Little Joe."

"He's the best."

"Funny thing about the French, having terrible barbers."

"I never thought of it that way."

One of the agents put his arm around Jackie Kasey's shoulder. "Jackie, Bill really wanted to introduce you, but he was running long. You know how it is."

The agent's name was Freddy Moyan and he had been Jackie's own personal friend and representative.

"Sure, Fred, I know how it is," Jackie Kasey said.

"Jackie, let me show you my watch," Lee Kalish said. He was a tall man with a lot of black hair and a white shirt with a modified Mr. B collar. He pulled back his monogrammed cuff to reveal a thin gold Patek watch with twin faces.

"Gee, Lee, that's terrific," Jackie Kasey said. He wondered what else he was supposed to say. So the watch had twin faces, so what. "What do you need two faces for?"

Lee Kalish smiled. A New York smile. A 1350 Sixth Avenue smile. A William Morris Agency 32nd floor variety department smile. A smile that headwaiters knew. Lee Kalish had logged a lot of hours in saloons in Vegas and Chicago and Miami Beach, casing singers, checking out comics, favoring them with that New York smile. "New York time and Vegas time," Lee Kalish said.

"Terrific," Jackie Kasey said.

Lee Kalish shot his cuffs and favored a keno

runner with his New York smile. "Honey, I'm Lee Kalish of the William Morris Agency."

The keno runner looked at Lee Kalish skeptically. Her breasts were too large and fatigue and resignation were etched into the paste of her face.

"Thought you'd like to be discovered," Lee Kalish said.

The girl turned and left without a word. It was just another pitch, she had heard better and she had heard worse.

"Catch your act later with the colored trumpet player," Lee Kalish called after her.

"Struck out that time, Lee," Barry Stern said.

"Too bad, Lee, she was totally titted," Mel Stavitz said.

Lee Kalish was undisturbed. He flashed his William Morris smile, the one with the teeth showing. "Fuck her," Lee Kalish said.

"Hey, let's go hear Corbett," Freddy Moyan said. Corbett Monica was a stand-up comic who was opening that night in the lounge at the Flamingo. "You want to come, Jackie?"

Jackie Kasey touched his throat and coughed. "My throat, I got a bad cold."

"You take care of that cold, Jackie," Lee Kalish said.

"Yeah, thanks, Lee," Jackie Kasey said.

The agents left Jackie there in the lobby. He wished Cosby's act had not gone long, tried to believe that was the reason he had not been introduced. He was glad he had not gone to see Corbett Monica. "What do I want to go hear another monologist for?" he said. "Corbett's okay, but you've got to grow. I've done monologues." He felt it necessary to repeat himself. "You've got to grow."

Growth. It was always on his mind. Anyone can do monologues. He had not scratched the surface with Brother JayJay yet. He would get it right. Just hang in there. Like Bob Hope. Even when Bob Hope was dying his balls were clanging in the basement. A comic had to have balls. Total balls. And keep it clean. Brother JayJay could only become a product if he kept it clean. What was it Buddy Hackett said? If the people want to hear the clean shit let them watch me on TV. That was fine for Buddy Hackett. He was already on TV, all the top talk shows. Jackie had not made it on Carson yet. That was for the future. When he had grown. When Brother JayJay was marketable. A product.

Jackie Kasey stood now under the lobby marquee waiting for his car to drive to the talk-show taping. He was dressed in a brown-leather Robin Hood outfit. The wet look. There was a man he knew in Los Angeles who gave him a special deal on his clothes. Semi-name clothes. A comic's clothes. Shit like this only performers wear. He was in Vegas. Headlining in the lounge. He knew Bill Cosby, he knew Tom Jones. It was a long way from Cleveland, even if Cosby had not introduced him from the stage.

His parents had owned a rooming house in Cleveland. He had used the rooming house in his act. Twenty-four rooms. The only rooming house in Cleveland you could smell in the Yellow Pages. A tough neighborhood. Stick-up men. What do you mean, stick-up, his father would say. Stick up Higbee's department store, they're making all the money. And listen, before you go hold up Higbee's, would you be interested in a little nine-by-twelve linoleum? Good material. It played when he was a monologist.

His brother was a policeman. Sometimes he made five hundred dollars a week. In the Depression. As a cop. No one asked how a cop made five hundred dollars a week. Not in Cleveland, where the police department was a bastion of collective bargaining. His brother made his stake in the police department and then retired to become a store detective. The pay was less but the hours were better and the reformers did not bother you. His brother knew a lot of people, people who used to help him out when he was a cop, and one of the people he knew gave Jackie a job in his clothing store. Even then Jackie was a clown, he was always joking the customers and the manager of the clothing store said he should be a comic. The manager knew a man who ran a resort in Mystic, Wisconsin, and the resort needed a social director and the manager recommended Jackie, his clerk, the clown. The resort was called Haven Inn and the social director's job paid twenty-one dollars a week plus room and board and all the nookie he could cop from the paying customers. Jackie was the lifeguard during the day and ran the volleyball games and the softball games and in the evening he emceed a show for the guests. He was twenty years old and he stayed at the Haven Inn in Mystic, Wisconsin, for a year. He lifted his material from Red Skelton and Uncle Miltie and all the other superstars on television and he would ad-lib with the guests, "Yeah, you were at the pool, but who was your wife with upstairs in the room, I'm not telling any stories, but I didn't see Manny the bartender pushing any gin fizzes between three and five."

They ate it up in Mystic, Wisconsin. He was a comic now and after a year he struck out for better things and the first stop was at Leo's Supper Club in Peoria, Illinois. A comic, an M.C., no volleyball, no softball, no lifeguarding, just his act, introduce the strippers with a little joke, something like, "Straight from her engagement at the Sisters of Mercy convent, Miss Lurleen." It was a tough crowd at Leo's, a shirt-sleeve crowd, beer drinkers with a lot of tattoos on their arms, and on opening night two guys in the audience got into a fight when he was onstage and one thing led to another until the first guy took out a gun and shot the second guy. Dead. It was a great way to begin a career and Jackie did not know how to get offstage, he had not learned how to handle a shooting at the Haven Inn in Mystic, Wisconsin, and he tried to bring out another stripper, "She's beautiful, she's twenty-one, she's an accountant," but the stripper would not come out and the boss was out front, putting towels around the dead guy's head, trying to stop the blood from dripping all over the floor and shouting at Jackie, "Get off, you stupid bastard, get off," and Jackie was saying, "That's okay, folks, we have these little differences of opinion every night," until finally the cops came and Leo's Supper Club closed down for the night.

It was like that on the Midwestern circuit. The joints were all owned by the Mob and the Mob guys were good. If they liked you, they would get on the telephone and call other Mob places and you would go from one Mob joint to another, $135 a week here, $150 a week there, staying in fleabag hotels where they changed the sheets every Monday and gave you one towel to last the week. The Mob guys all had a strange sense of humor. They would tell you how they beat a guy to death with a newspaper and did not leave a mark, a Jewboy, they would say, knowing you were a Jew, or they would say, "Hey, Jewboy, the guy we had here last week, he was really funny, you better be that funny," and then they would laugh and fold a newspaper and say, "Or else." The Mob guys were particularly funny at the Cardinal Club in Independence, Missouri. They would sit out in front and if they liked your act they would throw firecrackers at you onstage, just a little joke, if they didn't like you they would not throw the firecrackers. You went on wearing dirty underwear because the fleabags did not have laundry service and you had to go easy with the hecklers because the hecklers might be Mob guys and the Mob guys did not like the comic onstage saying to them, "Hey, let me check my brains, then we'll start out equal." The Mob places liked the humor broad, so broad that some of the joints thought that the Girl with the Itchy Twitchy routine was a bit sophisticated. "She has this sign. It says OPEN FOR BUSINESS. She hangs it on a lamp post." The audiences might not understand, the Mob guys would say, and you would switch into your Harold, the Homo Halfback routine.

"What do I like best about the sport? The showers, first the showers, and then the rubdowns. Some of the boys wear cups, but then they're missing all the fun in the pileups. Such fun in those pileups. No roughing penalties on me. You can't rough me up enough. The only time I ever got really angry was when a linebacker smudged my eyeliner. And he was so handsome."

Harold, the Homo Halfback was worth $150 a week in the Mob joints, but now Jackie was doing ten

grand a week in Vegas. With an act that didn't play.
Life was hard to figure out sometimes. A hundred and
eight grand last year and he couldn't figure out where
it had all gone. Three shrinks a week, one for him, one
for his wife and a little group thrown in, that cut into
the nut. And the gun-metal brown Mercedes 250 SL
that he was driving to the taping. But that was like the
clothes, a performer's car, a semi-name's car.

The M.C. on the television show was an avuncu-
lar-looking man named Ramsey Tait, who also wrote a
gossip column for one of the Vegas newspapers. Jackie
and Tait embraced.

"Jackie."

"Ramsey."

"How's the show."

"It's kind of like a love-in and a revival meeting
in the same show, Ramsey."

"I hear you're doing better business than some
of the main rooms, Jackie."

"That's right, Ramsey. I saw my shot and I had
to take it."

"I'm glad, Jackie."

"You know something, Ramsey? You and my
wife are the two people closest to me. The two who've
watched me grow and know what makes me tick."

"How is Roxy, Jackie?"

"She's always asking after you, Ramsey."

"Give her my best."

"The repeats are coming back, Ramsey."

"You've got to get the Vegas regulars, Jackie.
You can't make it on the tourists."

"The waiters don't call me Jackie any more.
They call me Brother JayJay."

"You can't make it without those people in this town, Jackie."

"They drum up the business, Ramsey."

"If the little people don't like you, they can kill you," Ramsey Tait said.

"They bad-rap you to the customers, you're dead."

"The little people." Tait put his arm around Jackie's shoulder. "Jackie, I've got you booked on with Gary Teale."

Jackie stopped growing. "I thought I was going to be on alone."

"Gary's a nice boy," Ramsey Tait said. "Sings with 'Voila Les Femmes' at the Dunes."

"A tit show," Jackie Kasey said bitterly.

"A nice boy," Tait said.

Jackie brushed a make-up puff over his face. He was clearly irritated. He had spent half a lifetime with tit shows in the Mob joints. He had worked with Elvis, he had worked with Frank, what did he need some fag from a tit show for. Tait walked onto the set.

"I thought I was going to be on alone," Jackie Kasey said. "Or maybe with Joan Rivers or Ed Ames. A superstar."

A young man came over and thrust his hand out toward Jackie. "Hi, Jackie. Gary Teale."

"Hi."

"Ramsey just asked me where I was from."

"Yeah."

"I guess I'm from L.A. as much as you can be from anyplace in this business. Right, Jackie?"

"Yeah."

"I guess you've got to say an entertainer's from a hotel room."

"Yeah." What did this fag know from hotel rooms in Erie, Pennsylvania, and Sioux City, Iowa.

Teale did not seem to know what else to say. He drifted on over toward Tait.

"They didn't tell me I was going to be on with that nipple," Jackie Kasey said. "I thought I was going to be on with a superstar. Who looks at the singer in a tit show. You can't see him for the boobs. They come to see the tits, not the fag."

The presumption of Gary Teale seemed to stagger Jackie Kasey. "You see that fag? Pretending he knew me."

Jackie Kasey cruised the lobby of the hotel after the taping. He was still annoyed at having to share the Ramsey Tait show with a singer from a boob show. It was bad enough, never having made Carson or Cavett, but to be on a local talk show that could scarcely be picked up in North Las Vegas with a shill for forty tits, that was too much.

"Hi, neighbor."

"Yeah, hi, how are you," Jackie Kasey said.

"Jerry Aronson." Jerry Aronson seemed to think Jackie should know who he was. He was standing by a roulette table with a stack of chips in his hand.

"How you hitting them?" Jackie Kasey said. His face was blank. He did not have a clue who the stranger was.

Though he was not chewing gum, Jerry Aronson moved his jaws constantly as if he were. "I bet you didn't know I was your neighbor," Jerry Aronson said.

"No shit?" Jackie Kasey said. He met all kinds in the casino and seemed resigned to let this one ride where it took him.

"No, I'm not shitting you," Jerry Aronson said. "You live on Lapeer, I live around the corner on Dayton. 210."

"Hey, Jerry, that's great. You live on Dayton, I live on Lapeer."

"And we're both in Vegas."

"Say hi to John Dunne. John, Jerry Adamson."

"Aronson."

"He's my neighbor," Jackie Kasey said to me. "210. What you doing up here, Jerry?"

"I commute."

"No shit?"

"No shit. I got a little perfume distributorship here. I spend the week here and the weekends back home in Beverly Hills."

"On Lapeer."

"Dayton. 210."

"That's great. Come and see the show."

"Not tonight, Jackie. I got to meet some guys. Tomorrow, the first show."

"Hey, great, I'll tell the maître d' to expect you."

"That's great, neighbor." They did not seem to know how to take the conversation any further. Finally Jerry Aronson feinted like a boxer and nudged Jackie's arm. "I figure my dog shits on your lawn, I got to say hello."

"You tell him he can shit on my lawn any time, Jerry."

"No shit?"

"No shit."

TEN

Artha was depressed. It had been a bad day at the Manhattan Beauty College. She blamed it on the recession. That fucking Nixon. She wasn't political, she had never registered to vote. Register to vote and she might be called to jury duty and if she were called to jury duty it would be hard to work. Although it might be nice, when a judge asked what she did, to say, "I blow a lot of guys." That would shake up His Honor. Fuck him. And Nixon, too. There was a recession, he was in the White House, he should have fixed it. Artha blamed Nixon for getting busted. It was the first time she had been busted since Milwaukee, and that was for carrying reds. This time the bust was for hooking. It was Nixon's recession, it was his fault. When she applied to the Manhattan Beauty College, she had thought she would only hook on weekends. That would keep her going and leave her time to study on week nights. But the recession had hit Vegas so hard that she was now forced to work during the week. She was not doing her homework, she had begun to cut classes. It was difficult to take a three o'clock date and then get up for an eight o'clock class. It was better to cut the class altogether than to be tired and make a mistake in bluing or tinting. She was tired all the time now. The nights were longer. There were so few high rollers around that the pits were not coming through with the steady good tricks and she had started to cruise. Because of the recession. And cruising was how she got busted. Right off a blackjack table at the Land-mark.

Artha had stopped to play a hand of twenty-one. She did not gamble much. She just wanted to rest her feet. And be on display. A single girl at a blackjack table at three in the morning. Even the rubes could figure that out. She had been cruising since midnight with no luck. The secret of cruising was to keep moving. Caesars first, then the Tropicana, then the Sands. No luck. No more than two drinks in any casino. Stay for more than two drinks without making a connection and hotel security begins to get nervous. The hotels draw a very fine line. They like the girls available for the roller who wants a pop, but then they don't want the casino to look like a lamppost. So two drinks and move on. Artha had talked to a lot of guys. Lookers, talkers, guys who wanted to negotiate. The nice thing about working out of the pits was that there was no negotiating. That was all fixed beforehand. A hundred dollars, cash or chips. Cruising was different. There was always some dude who got his rocks off negotiating. A hundred to fifty, fifty to thirty. At three o'clock in the morning with no hits, even thirty looked good. Then the guy would say no, he thought not, it was a little steep. Fuck him. That kind of guy was trouble. When she first got to Vegas, before she made her connections in the pits, she had always cruised with a friend. If she got a trick, she would tell her friend his room number. If she was not down in an hour, give the room a call. There were guys who liked to work a girl over, a little punch in the tit to liven up the evening. So call in an hour to see if I'm okay. It was better to be safe than sorry.

Artha was tired at the Landmark. Her feet hurt and she did not feel like moving on to the Sahara. That was her mistake; she did not keep moving. She looked up and saw the cop beckoning to her. She had never seen him before, but she knew he was not just another john. Johns never beckon. They always ask for a match or the time or say what a nice night it is or how lucky they feel. Only the vice crook their fingers. When a dude snaps his finger, beckons with his hand and wears a small American flag in his lapel, a working girl can be sure it's the vice.

She went along. A girl always went along. It was not smart to cause trouble. She wanted to work the Landmark again and if she caused a scene she never would. Hotel security would be on her ass before she got through the automatic door. Nor did the vice want to cause a scene. The hotel would disapprove and the hotel had too much juice downtown. The only difference between getting busted and walking out of the hotel with a trick was that she did not take the cop's arm. Nobody could tell what was happening except hotel security and some of the people in the pits. No one seemed to notice, not even a blackjack dealer who had turned a fifty-dollar pop over to her the night before. Before the recession, the dealer used to turn her on to a couple of tricks a week. Artha had never turned any money over to him. He had balled her a few times and there was one thing about him that she particularly liked. He had never asked to come to her apartment. She would have let him, but he never asked. He lived in a two-bedroom apartment on the west side of the Strip and sometimes after a date she would play a couple of hands at his table and he would say that if she was not busy he got off in a half-hour or so. That was all, nothing more. Sometimes she would say yes and other times when she was tired or had had too much action, she would smile and say no. "You're at the end of a long line," she would say, and he would laugh and deal her another hand. He never paid. That was part of the bargain. But she did not turn him down too often. Times were too tough and the supply far exceeded the demand. If a girl wanted to make a living, she could not tell a good contact in the pits to go take a cold shower every time he hinted around for a freebie.

Only her contacts got the free pussy. All the other locals paid. Artha had worked out an elaborate pay scale for the locals. She let a dealer go for a "quarter," or twenty-five dollars, a pit boss for a half, or fifty. It was a flat hundred for the casino or hotel manager. There was one hotel manager who anted up a hundred and a half every time. The extra fifty was so the girl would not wash him. He had a phobia about being washed. It seemed to him too professional. The money did not make it professional, only the washing. That was how Artha had lost him as a trick. She had washed his joint first thing. He let her finish, but then wadded the two bills into her purse and dismissed her before they got anything going. It was a long time before Artha even worked his hotel. She was afraid that because she had soaped his joint he had put the word out for hotel security to lean on her if she ever came in. It was too bad, but she washed everyone, she did not care who he was. She said it was going to be difficult for her if she ever got married, because on her wedding night she was sure to take a washcloth, some soap and warm water, and that would not look right. But it had paid off. She had only got the clap once and that was when she was in high school in Wisconsin. She was almost sure she had caught it from a boy named Walter Keenan, whose brother was a Dominican priest and whose mother was active in the St. Vincent de Paul Society.

Artha often wondered how she had only managed to catch the clap once, even with all the washing. She had played around with a very rough group in Milwaukee, spades mainly, numbers people, pimps, second-story men, some dealers in reds. She had never taken to drugs. She simply did not like them. "They just don't agree with me," she said. She had taken up with a black pimp after her baby was born. There was a black girl in the maternity ward with her and the pimp had come to see her a couple of times, but he had spent most of his time talking to Artha. She had never balled a black man before, although at that time she never called them blacks. In the part of Milwaukee where she was brought up, blacks were "niggers," and it surprised her when she got out of the hospital and began going with the pimp that the blacks called each other "nigger," although they did not much like it if a white person did. She went with the pimp for several months and he bought her clothes and paid for her apartment and one day when he asked her to do a white friend a favor and work a house in Antigo, Wisconsin, she said why not.

Antigo is in the potato and lumber country and the house was a two-girl affair and she was expected to service anyone who came through the door. The other girl did not seem to be around and the madam said the other girl was having her period, but a couple of days later Artha learned that a lumberjack had laid open the girl's skull with an axe handle. It was an accident, he was drunk, the girl would live. Artha was not reassured. She had arrived in Antigo on the bus on a Tuesday and was back in Milwaukee Friday afternoon, missing the big weekend rush in the lumber country. But in the slow middle of the week in Antigo, Tuesday night, Wednesday night and Thursday night, she had serviced thirty-one potato farmers and lumberjacks, and that seemed more than adequate payment for the clothes and the apartment the pimp had given her.

She took up with another pimp, who brought her to Chicago and set her up in a cheap hotel on the ten-hundred block of North Clark Street, three dollars a night for the room, and every trick paid the three, so the hotel did not mind the heavy traffic. There was a coin-operated television set in the room, twenty-five cents for a half-hour of TV time, and she balled the night clerk for a roll of quarters in order to watch "The Man from U.N.C.L.E." and her favorites between tricks. The night clerk's name was Opatashu and he had cancer of the rectum and he shit out of his side into a little bag attached to his waist. But he was straight, on, off, no tricks, no gimmicks, not like some of the guys she met on North Clark Street, especially the one with the hot plate. The john with the hot plate would carry it around with him and when he picked up a girl, he would fry up a couple of eggs in her room, dump the

eggs on her pussy and then eat them with a plastic knife
and fork. That was all, nothing more, except the yolk
from the sunny-side-up crusting in her pubes. Opatashu
died while she was on North Clark Street and she went
to his funeral. It was something to do, she did not like
to waste her quarters on the game shows on TV in the
afternoon and the local cooking show reminded her of
the john with the hot plate. The assistant manager and
the housekeeper of the hotel were at the cemetery, and
it struck Artha that it was a sad way to die, cancer of
the asshole, poor Opatashu, no place even to crap out
of in the end, attended at death only by a fag, a hooker
and a spade maid.

Chicago was the furthest east she had ever been.
She wanted to see New York someday, but the place
that really interested her was Buffalo. No reason. She
just liked the name. She did not even know anyone
there. She was like that about cities. If the name was
nice, the city was probably nice. Another city she
thought would be an all-right place was Macon,
Georgia. Once she had tricked a john from Macon. He
was in the dental-supply business and was in Vegas for
a convention and told her he wanted "the W.F.W."

"What's that?"

"The whole fucking works," he had said. "It's
a Macon expression."

W.F.W. She liked that and eased it into a conversation whenever she got the chance. In a restaurant
she would order a schnitzel with the W.F.W. and if the
waiter looked at her strangely she would say, "The
whole fucking works, it's a Macon expression." That
was a nice thing about Vegas; the waiters never batted
an eye. They had heard it all, the W.F.W. When a trick

took her to dinner, she would immediately call for the wine list. She always ordered wine by the number on the list. "Number sixty-nine," she would say. It was cute the way the waiters always got the joke.

"May I recommend instead Number sixty-five," they would say.

"That's four short," she would say.

She had been in Vegas five years. Long enough to learn all the tricks. She free-lanced for a while, until she met a couple of bell captains. But the trouble with hooking through the bell captains or the cab drivers was that they took 40 percent. Off the top. Working out of the pits was not as steady, but there was less overhead. Better free pussy to every dealer in town than 40 percent. The bar men got to know her. That was important. They would tell her when the vice was making a sweep through the hotel and she would disappear into the ladies' room. Once while she was cruising the Sands the heat made a swing through the casino and when she disappeared into the can an old broad in a silver pants suit offered fifty dollars to watch her take a leak. Artha had to take a leak anyway, so it was no problem. That was another thing she liked about Vegas; it was possible to turn a profit just by taking a piss.

She kept moving, she never got busted. Until the recession. Nixon's recession. Not that she ever got careless. It was too easy to run afoul of the heat. One of the first things she did when she got to Vegas was to get herself a bail bondsman. Just in case she did get busted. The bail bondsman's name was Bill Parsons and most of the hookers on the Strip used him. It was easy to find him in the Yellow Pages. His slogan was, "I'll Get You Out of Jail and Onto the Street." She gave Bill Parsons a fifty-dollar cashier's check so that in case she did get busted he could bail her right out. And she got herself a lawyer. Again just in case. The charge in a hooking bust was usually vag loitering. It was just a harassing tactic the vice used to keep cruising in the casinos within reason. The vice would never bust a girl when she was with a trick. There was no knowing how much juice the trick had. He could be an optometrist, but then again he could be the chief of police of some burg in Arkansas. Or one of the People. Or someone with a fifty-thousand-dollar line of credit at the Sahara. The kind of people it was best not to mess with.

It was just Artha's bad luck that she was alone. And that it was after midnight. If she had been busted before midnight she could have made bail and been back in the casinos within the hour. But after midnight you have to spend the night in the tank. She made her one call to Bill Parsons and he said he would get her out the next morning. She settled in for the night. Or what was left of it. In knee boots and black-velvet hot pants. The only excitement was when a spade tried to pinch her sausage-curl wig. Artha told the spade she would get a kick in the cunt if she was not careful. It was tough enough to cruise in the recession without a boot up the twat. The spade got the message.

Artha was out by eight the next morning. She gave Bill Parsons another fifty-dollar check to cover the bond for the next time she was busted, and went home to bed. She would not have to appear in court. Vag loitering was a misdemeanor and the cases were always dismissed. But the lawyer cost a hundred, and with Bill Parsons' fifty, that meant a cee and a half. And no tricks to cover it. She would have to cruise again that night. Which is what caused all the trouble at the Manhattan Beauty College.

The problem was that she had missed the lessons about applying the solution for a permanent. Because she was working nights and cutting classes the next day. At school she was now on the floor and over the past week she had picked up $7.85 in tips while doing $21.50 worth of work. What she had learned, she had learned well. She was good at dyes and tints and was now into cuts, practicing on the wigs and falls that the Manhattan Beauty College kept on blocks for the students to work on. The customers at the college were all women who worked downtown, older women mostly, the kind who wanted rinses and permanents and wanted them done cheaply. Artha had done a rinse and a tint that morning and she had performed both jobs meticulously. She was not fast, but she was thorough, and speed would come later. What was important now was learning how to do the job right. Everything was going well until this old broad in bifocals came in and demanded a permanent. Artha was the only girl free on the floor. She did not have permanents down yet, but it was worth a try. She put on too much solution. The woman began to complain. Artha got flustered. She was tired, she began to make mistakes. She realized how little sleep she had been getting. First the night in the tank, then last night, trying to make up for it, with a man from Chicago who dealt in pork futures. She had spent the evening with him at the crap tables at the Riviera and then when she finally got him to his room he could not get it up. She worked on him for two hours, until four-thirty in the morning. The

john was in for a hundred, but when he could not make
it, he demanded fifty back. She had first told him to go
fuck himself and then she remembered the night in the
tank and returned the fifty. Two nights in the tank were
two too many. And now this old bitch was complaining
about the solution. It was burning her scalp, it was
splitting the hair ends. Mr. Luigi ordered Artha off the
floor and began to soothe the customer. Her permanent
would be free. Mr. Luigi would perform it himself. That
old bitch. Fuck her. Fuck the recession. Fuck Nixon.

2

Recession notes. Empty rooms over the Fourth
of July weekend. Tourist volume down thirty-five percent. The slots at Caesars down eight percent, table
action down nineteen percent. Eight million dollars in
uncollected gambling debts. Hotels tightening up on the
comp.

Quotes: "The high rollers are declining. Take
Mr. Average Manufacturer. A couple of years ago he
would have maybe three to four hundred thousand dollars' worth of stock and he could risk ten thousand
dollars at the tables and sell some stock if he lost. Now
his stock is worth maybe eighty thousand dollars and
he can't afford to gamble. The economy did him in."

"It's Howard Hughes that done it. Trying to
turn Vegas into some kind of desert Disneyland. *Vegas.*
Miniature golf and all that shit. Bugsy would turn over
in his grave. Try putting hookers in Disneyland and see
how long Mom would keep taking the kiddies to see
Mickey Mouse. It's the same principle."

"Someone should build a wax statue of Bugsy Siegel, then they should put the statue in a hotel room, splatter the walls with catsup and machine-gun bullets and charge the tourists a dollar each for a look at the city's history."

3

Marvin Berlin talking:

"I suppose you can say that there's a kind of generation gap in the type of games people play. Now your older fellow, he's probably a crap player. There's a reason for that, of course. The country's locked up so tight these days the younger people don't really have access to the better game of craps, so they really don't understand all the subtleties of the game, the variations and the combinations. They don't have the opportunity to learn. I won't say it's a bad thing for the country that there are so few young crap players, I mean, of course, *good* crap players, but I think it's a bad thing for gambling. I mean, I think the country's a poorer place for the fact that we don't have any more buffalo. So closing down your better game is killing off a whole new generation of crap players, and to me that means the end of the species. So you see what I mean by the buffalo.

"Now when a dealer graduates from here, he is by no means an accomplished dealer. What he needs is seasoning. He needs to go out and bump heads with the gambling public. But just in case things do get out of hand, every hotel has what we call here in Vegas an 'eye in the sky.' That's a two-way mirror built into the ceiling of the casino, where an executive of the hotel can

check the action at every one of the tables without being
detected by the players. Now, some of the eyes in the
sky around town have television cameras up there and
they can pinpoint the action on every table and beam
it back closed circuit to the manager's office. Generally
you don't have a man up there all the time, but if you
suspect something's going on, or if it's a really big game
with a lot on the table, you send somebody up to take
a look.

"I remember working in a casino once where
they thought money was missing off the table and they
didn't have an eye in the sky. And the way the building
was constructed there was no way to put one in. But
they felt they were being shorted on this table and they
felt they knew who the dealer was who was shorting
them and they felt they had to do something. The guy
they suspected was working day shift and so on the
graveyard shift, you know, that's the middle of the
night, they came in and screwed a mirror onto the
ceiling. Nothing behind the mirror, there was no room,
it was just a con. But they left some plaster on this guy's
table and when he comes in to work the next morning,
he picked a piece of plaster off his table, saw the new
mirror and he knew the jig was up. He quit right there
and that was it.

"In a lot of places you know when the man is
up there in the eye in the sky. When I was working at
the Dunes, I always knew if the man was upstairs. You
see, the chandelier began to move, not much, just
enough so that you knew someone was walking around
up there. And then if you could see the chandelier
moving you could look and see shadows behind the
mirror. So you knew you were on candid camera.

"And then there's another little wrinkle. Some of the joints put video tape machines up there in the eye so that if they smell something bad they can put you on instant replay. And keep running it until they find out what's bothering them.

"It's not without its funny side. Last week at the International, the guy in the eye dropped a telephone. It went right through the mirror, shattered the glass and landed on a blackjack table. There were seven people sitting there and it sounded like someone was shot. One thing you can be sure of, if there was anything funny going on, it sure as hell stopped."

4

I saw a lot of Artha. Afternoons, when she got home from the Manhattan Beauty College, she would walk her two chihuahuas, Mario and Maria, and then if she did not have a date until later in the evening, she would give me a call. "Want to eat some pussy?"

"Not particularly."

"How about some chili?"

We ate often in a Mexican restaurant downtown. There was something reassuringly county-line about Fremont Street after the alpaca cardigans and varicose veins of the Strip. Downtown seemed the last refuge of the duck's-ass haircut. Kids dragged the main with squirrel tails bobbing from their radio antennas. The bars were full of three-hundred-pound bikers drinking beer from the bottle and women whose features had long since been swallowed by their jowls; both shared that slack fatty tissue nourished exclusively by a diet of cornflakes and Dr. Pepper. In the topless places, the go-go girls wore silver-sequined pasties on limp breasts crosshatched with veins and maternity stretch marks. The dildo and vibrator shops all accepted Master Charge and Bank Americard, and in the men's room of a casino at First and Fremont there were six different prophylactic dispensers, offering the customer a choice among Tops, Con-Form, Prestige, Linger, Sus-Tain and Pro-Long. It was all so down-home, so divorced from the impacted venality of the Strip. Perhaps for this reason, Fremont Street seemed to jog Artha's memory, to erase from her mind the inroads made by the recession and by the nose suckers. I remember standing with her one night outside the El Cortez Casino watching an old woman in a wheelchair selling Chiclets and chewing gum and key chains made from dice. The woman had no legs, just scarred leather pads attached to the stumps of her knees. Hanging from the arms of her wheelchair were two signs. The first said, "I receive no form of public assistance," and the second, "Let me be your Lady Luck tonight."

I found the sight so grotesque that I had to avert my eyes, but Artha continued to stare at the legless woman. "She reminds me of my Home Ec teacher in the eighth grade," she said finally. "She wasn't a crip, but she looked like that broady. She helped me sew my first formal. Green nylon organza. Strapless. With a bolero effect."

"Did you have a good time?"

The reverie ended. "I gave Wallace Gould a hand job."

We saw a lot of porno movies. She claimed to

have made one that she had never seen, and the possibility of seeing herself on screen was always her pretext for
making me take her to whatever skinner was playing in
town. She actually got a kick out of watching people
fuck on camera, and an even bigger kick out of being
the only woman in the audience. Her comments on the
action showed a certain gutter wisdom. "Did you ever
see a guy in a dirty movie who didn't have a tattoo?"
she would say, or "Life is too short to fuck anyone who
wears jockey shorts." Her every day seemed to involve
some fantasy kinship with celebrity. She called all the
entertainers in the Strip showrooms only by their first
names ("I'm catching Englebert's midnight show," she
would say, or "Let's hit Dean's opening"), she was
sharply critical, on professional grounds, of "Jane's"
performance as the prostitute in *Klute* ("That broady
could never pussy whip anybody") and she tried never
to make a date during the hour-and-a-half "The Dick
Cavett Show" was on the air. (I once asked her why she
preferred Cavett to Carson and she replied, "Johnny
plays the Sahara.") From eleven-thirty to one, she
would sit in her apartment watching Cavett, simultaneously crocheting or reading books about the Mafia.
Occasionally there would be a guest on the show she
had known professionally, and in the most matter-of-
fact way she would detail the guest's sexual idiosyncra-
sies. "Quick pop," she would say, or (and this was the
most baroque) "He got turned on by the heartbreak-of-
psoriasis commercial."

What was most disconcerting about my relationship with Artha was that it was recognized as pimp-
ship, and nothing more, by Strip headwaiters. Disconcerting because I had a higher view of myself, a view,

in light of my other relationships in Vegas, that was
perhaps unjustified. One night we decided to have dinner at Del Prado, the expensive French restaurant at
the Monaco. ("Expensive" and "French" are relative
terms when discussing the cuisine of the Strip; all the
food tastes as if it were cooked in the morning and
placed on a steam tray for the rest of the day.) The
headwaiter was wearing a tuxedo with black piping and
a blue ruffled shirt and there was enough spray on his
hair to keep it in place even under the full force of a
desert gale.

"*Notre spécialité ce soir est les grenouilles proven-
çales,*" the headwaiter said. A rich Gallic smile deco-
rated his face. "That's frog's legs with tomato sauce.
We hold the garlic."

"I'll have a shot of milk on the rocks, crème de
cocoa back," Artha said.

"*Certainement, mademoiselle,*" the headwaiter
said. "*Et pour monsieur?*"

"A glass of O.J."

"Over ice?"

"*Oui.*"

The headwaiter seemed to hesitate for a moment. Pointedly ignoring me, he said to Artha, "The
gentleman at Table Fourteen . . ."

The gentleman from Table 14 had pearl-gray
hair piled in swirls and eddies atop his head and the
caps on his teeth were just a shade too big. He smiled
at Artha, made a circle of his thumb and forefinger,
then cocked it into a pistol.

"A real tiger," Artha said.

"The gentleman wonders if you would care to
join him," the headwaiter said to Artha.

"*Et monsieur aussi?*" I said.

The headwaiter regarded me as if I were Iceberg
Slim. "*Mademoiselle seulement.*"

Artha smiled benignly at the gentleman at Table
14. "Fuck him," she said. And then to the headwaiter:
"Two specials, easy on the tomato sauce."

In the newspapers I kept track of the conventions that were in town. The National Electrical Con-
tractors Association. The Association of Consulting
Engineers. The Bank Public Relations and Marketing
Association. The Architectural Aluminum Manufac-
turers Association. The Independent Bankers Association of America. The Society of Mining Engineers of
AIME. There were 25,000 hotel and motel rooms in
Vegas and the surrounding communities and in those
25,000 hotel and motel rooms stayed the quarter of a
million convention delegates who had visited Vegas
over the past year. To Artha 250,000 convention delegates meant 250,000 possible tricks. Where there was a
convention there was a hospitality suite and what better
place to make a connection than in a hospitality suite.
The problem was getting past hotel security and that
was where I came in.

I had a press pass.

5

The Yamaha International Dealers convention
was headquartered at the Frontier. Yamaha. The motorcycle people. The *Japanese* motorcycle people. Japanese—that was the operative word. Correction—the
nonoperative word. Yamaha's ad guys from N.W. Ayer

passed the message from the home islands: no Jap jokes at the convention. No *banzai*s, no *kamikaze*s, no *ah so*s. No Japanese calligraphy on the artwork. The economic miracle, okay, Pearl Harbor, forget it. The Yamaha convention was a $400,000 operation, $250,-000 in air fares alone for the 2,700 dealers and loved ones, plus fifty big ones for the convention itself. The rest was for incidentals. Five free drinks for every registrant. Free keno tickets. Door prizes. A grand prize of a free trip around the world.

Ah so.

The average Yamaha dealer was thirty-nine years old and married. Nearly a quarter of the dealers worked with their wives. Papa-*san* and Mama-*san* stores on the outskirts of large urban areas. Example: Phil's in Azusa. Most of the dealers dealt in multiple bike lines, usually Yamaha and BSA, seldom Yamaha and Honda, that was frowned upon, that was Macy's and Gimbel's time. This was the fourth year Yamaha had held its convention in Vegas and the morning line on the Yamaha dealers was that they were good spenders, they came to play, they had peckers. Which is what Artha was counting on. A thirty-nine-year old pecker without his wife.

She tried on seven wigs before deciding on a black Afro number to wear to the Yamaha hospitality suite. Plus knee-high white vinyl boots, a white vinyl miniskirt and a crocheted burnt-orange top. Plus four jade rings on the first two fingers of either hand. Plus an over-the-shoulder needlepoint bag containing among other artifacts two French ticklers and a Sony vibrator for the more recherché Oriental tastes, an aerosol container of Binaca and a small tube of K-Y.

"How do I look," she said on the way over to
the Frontier.

"Stunning."

"I'm going to blow a Jap."

I signed in at the registration desk and was given
two plastic name tags. On Artha's I wrote in grease
pencil, ARTHA—VEGAS. She pinned it directly over her
left nipple, where it jiggled like the tassle on a stripper's
pastie. I was beginning to get the feeling that she was
going to come on with the boys from Yamaha like a
Harley chopper.

I lost her moments after we hit the hospitality
suite. The room was jammed with Seagram Seven &
Seven drinkers and small Japanese gentlemen in dark
suits, looking like islands in a sea of checkered double
knits.

"That MX is a damn fine bike, Mr. Hakishima,
it'll sweep Honda right out of Tucson."

Mr. Hakishima bowed and smiled.

"We got this street in Tucson, it's called, you
know, Speedway, it's the most famous street in
Arizona, and I want to tell you something, you don't
see a fucking Honda, no, sir, you don't."

"I go for the Mini-Enduro."

"Shit, I don't know, it's not enough bike."

"But what we're talking about here is the family
bike."

"I don't think you can call your bike a family
machine."

"That's where I think you're mistaken."

"No, I think your bike is a luxury item."

"Like a second car?"

"Shit, in this economy, a second car is a luxury

item. That's what makes your bike market so important."

The crowd swirled around the room. Occasionally I caught a glimpse of Artha's burnt-orange blouse.
She always seemed surrounded by a quorum of Yamaha
dealers. I tried to press closer to her. She was munching
on a plate of canapés. A Japanese speared a cocktail
frankfurter and handed it to her. "Some mustard,
please?" he asked.

"The W.F.W.," she said.

The Japanese looked bewildered.

"The whole fucking works," Artha said. "It's a
Macon expression."

Before I could reach her, I was intercepted by
one of the Yamaha ad men. He was tall, thin, sagging
a little in the face and very sincere. Light-green shirt,
darker green alpaca cardigan, poplin safari pants. He
talked not so much well as constantly. There would be
2,700 people at the Yamaha cocktail party at the Convention Center, he said, figure ten square feet per person, 27,000 square feet in all, did you know that, why,
these fellows have an equation for everything, they
really know their onions, that's why Vegas is such a
great town to hold a convention. You take your music.
A group like The Kids Next Door, why, they wanted
$3,000 just to appear at the convention and I told them
that's a little steep, you can get the Young Americans
for not much more than that, so you know what we did,
we got a group right here in Vegas, the Ambassadors,
fifty bodies for $350 *plus* they supply their own uni-
forms, that's seven dollars per head, and right there
you're talking about cost per thousand and that's the
kind of language we understand. Now you take noise-

makers, I don't want to make a decision on noisemak-
ers, if I give everyone a noisemaker, that could cost me
$425, and believe me, that's the kind of cost that will
chew you to death. The thing about Yamaha you got
to remember is that they're the nicest people in the
world to work with, it's a three-million-dollar account,
and the only stipulation they make is no Jap jokes, and
from their position I can see the point of that. It's
twenty-five years now, they've paid their dues, and I bet
that if you don't have a bike, well, then, I bet your TV
set is a Sony, you've got something Japanese in your
house, it's the workmanship, those little people care and
that is why it is a delight to work with them.

Ah so.

I spotted Artha again. The group around her
had thinned out and she was licking the mustard off a
toy hot dog, listening intently to two men who seemed
unaware of her presence. I edged closer. One man's
name tag said, TEX HARPER—COLORADO SPRINGS and
the other's ROY ROWE—TULSA.

"It's a blessing in a way, Roy."

"Any pain, Tex?"

"Not so much since the stroke. That's one thing
you can say for a stroke, it takes care of the pain."

"Last year, just last year, May was here in
Vegas."

"She had it even then."

"I never would have known it."

"She knew."

"Cancer."

"Eating right through her bones."

"Damn fine lady, May."

"Hasn't hit her vital organs yet. That's why the doctor said it would take a long time."

"I can see why the stroke's a blessing."

"She cries all the time."

"She knows, then?"

"She's afraid. She won't let me out of her sight. When I've got to go to the bathroom, I've got to tell her how long it will take and she times me."

"Can't even read the newspaper."

"Can't even get excited about the new line."

"You should try the Mini-Enduro, though."

Artha finished her hot dog and wiped her hands delicately on a cocktail napkin. "You want to hear a cute story?" she said to Tex Harper.

Tex Harper looked blankly at Artha.

She raised her right hand and showed him one of the jade rings. "See this ring?" she said. "There's a cute story behind it."

"It's very pretty."

"Jade."

"Tell Tex a cute story," Roy Rowe said.

"Well, this is a hundred-fifty-dollar ring and I got it for fifty dollars," Artha said.

"That sounds like a real bargain," Tex Harper said.

"I'd like a bargain like that," Roy Rowe said.

Artha smiled and batted her false eyelashes. "You've got to be a broady to get my kind of bargain."

"How's that?" Roy Rowe said. He seemed to have forgotten all about May and was deep into Artha's rap. I watched, mesmerized, fearing the worst.

"Well, see, I've got this john, he's in the wholesale jewelry business, and I liked this ring and he said he would give me a discount, you know, if I let him give it to me in the ass. Up the chocolate freeway, you know?"

"I see," Roy Rowe said.

"I see," Tex Harper said.

"That's a hundred off the price of the ring right there," Artha said.

"A discount."

"That's right." She took a cheese puff and popped it into her mouth. "Now, here's the cute part. He got out the Vaseline and lathered it all over my ass, we were going to do it dog style, right? Well, he poked me in one cheek and then he poked me in the other cheek, he couldn't get it in, and then he came before he got it in my crack and I got the ring for fifty dollars. He really laughed. He told me I really drove a hard bargain. So that's the story of how I got my ring."

She smiled brightly at Tex Harper and Roy Rowe.

"It's a cute story, isn't it?" Artha said.

6

I left Artha in the hospitality suite still telling cute stories and went home to my apartment. I needed to feed on some fantasies of my own, anything to erase the grotesqueries of the evening. I thought of driving to Los Angeles, I thought of driving to Tucson, but in the end I just turned on "The Dick Cavett Show." During that season, I could not watch a talk show without fantasizing. What I fantasized about depended on my mood, the weather, anything. I would talk to Dick about my sixty-two-home-run season, my Oscar, my

Nobel Prize. I am wry, I am angry, I am asked to come back again. Someone punches the applause button and I walk off, hand lifted high in the peace signal. As befits a star, I always do a solo gig; the real stars do not stick around to chatter with rock personalities or contract starlets with pictures opening that week at selected theaters and drive-ins.

The fact is, however, that I would never be a talk-show regular. My voice on the air gets high and squeaky and my stammer prevents me from indulging in articulate patter. Like all stammerers, I have my own Distant Early Warning System. I know what hard consonants are difficult for me to say—two-syllable words beginning with a *c* or a *t* are an impossibility—and I can always think of some synonym four or five words in advance; for "connection" I will substitute "link," for "together" I will use "with each other," and for a film "director," the "man who makes the picture." The effect of this DEW System is to give my speech an odd, jerky pattern, as if I am simultaneously translating from another language.

And so I fantasize. I transferred myself that night of the cute story into the seat on Cavett's right. I was a .400 hitter who had written a book attacking the baseball establishment, not a rag arm like Jim Bouton who had lost his fast-ball, but a superstar, the best natural hitter since Shoeless Joe Jackson, the best sportsman-writer since Papa.

"What did Commissioner Kuhn say to you when he read the galleys?"

"Well, Dick, he told me if I published the book he would bar me from the game. Something about it being detrimental to the image of baseball. And I want to say something right here, Dick: I love this game. It's my life."

"So despite this threat you decided to go ahead and publish?"

"I had to."

"It was a matter of principle?"

"Dick, I think a ball player has the same right of free speech as two hundred million other Americans. So I said to Bowie Kuhn, 'Commissioner, have you ever read the Constitution of the United States of America?' "

"Good point."

"I think so."

"But don't you think you're betraying your teammates and friends by trafficking in the secrets of the locker room?"

A deep breath, a telegenic smile. "Dick, I think if Thomas Wolfe of Asheville told you that a writer's only loyalty was to himself, you wouldn't question it. You think of me as a .400 hitter. I think of myself as a writer who also happens to be a .400 hitter."

I sat on my bed watching the tube, tears in my eyes. I was in the groove. There was a commercial and then the camera was back on Cavett.

"My next guest . . ."

The telephone rang. It was Artha. She had made a connection at the Yamaha hospitality suite. A hundred dollars and breakfast. I was too tired to ask whether the trick was Tex Harper or Roy Rowe.

ELEVEN

The plastic namecard read, HI, I'M LESTER TOUHY, O.P., NATIONAL ASSOCIATION OF INDUSTRY EDUCATION COUNCILS. I kept my eyes on Lester Touhy, the Passionist. He was wearing black alligator loafers with little tassels, black serge pants with flare pockets and no cuffs, a black dickey and a white dog collar and a double-knit double-breasted midnight-blue blazer with gold buttons in the shape of tiny anchors. Lester Touhy, the Passionist, seemed the perfect priest to send to a Vegas convention. Goggle glasses and razor-cut hair modishly styled over the ears, but still a dog collar, a Passionist at ease in the secular world of fund raising, given to Wild Turkey, Big Six and ten the hard way. I tried to imagine confessing to Lester Touhy. "Bless me, Father, for I have sinned."

"That's cool."

All the while I was staring at Lester Touhy, O.P., Jackie Kasey was whispering in my ear. We were having breakfast at the coffee shop in the hotel and he was trying to fix me up with a date. His girl friend was a keno runner at the Taj Mahal and her roommate

shoveled sundaes at the ice-cream shop at Oasis, nineteen years old, name of Teddi, and she'll suck you and
fuck you. I demurred. Not that I had anything against
sucking or fucking. It was the nineteen that was bother-
some. And so I concentrated on Lester Touhy.

The thing is, Father, I'm uncomfortable with
women born after VJ Day. There is nothing that can
make the sexual imperative die quicker than trying to
explain to a teenager with great tits the difference between VE Day and VJ Day. I want them to remember
the Battle of the Bulge and Colin Kelly and that Lucky
Strike green went to war. Or at least to have heard of
the *Enola Gay.* If they were born after the *Enola Gay,*
it's not likely yet that they cry without reason in tax-
icabs or have distorted cervixes. I just find it easier to
cope with women who do. Women who had abortions
in an apartment two blocks from the last stop on the
Jersey side of the Hudson tube. That's a different thing
altogether from a free clinic scrape. Women who cook
tripe à la mode in the middle of the night because ribs
broken by a former lover hurt. Women who check
themselves into Cedars Sinai at four in the morning
with a severe pelvic infection that turns out to be an
acute case of the clap. Women who go to Grenada alone
to get over a love affair and end up sleeping with a
sixty-seven-year old remittance man and ex-con who
did four years for embezzling from a print shop in
Meriden, Connecticut.

What I am trying to say, Father, is that I find
it nearly impossible to be with it. I smoke a lot of dope
and like the Rolling Stones and wear faded blue jeans
and Levi jackets, but the jeans are faded in the washing
machine with Clorox and Downy fabric softener. How

do I explain to a nineteen-year-old that I like to walk through cemeteries and compose suicide notes and listen to quiet-voiced women talk about ovarian cysts? Or that I like to sing the Gregorian chant at the top of my lungs when driving on the freeways, *Credo in unum Deo,* not so much out of belief but because I like the melody, it does a lot more for me than "Light My Fire." *Sanctus, sanctus, sanctus Dominus Deus sabaoth, pleni sunt coeli et terra, gloria tua,* an oldie but goody, tops in pops for nineteen hundred years.

Lester Touhy, O.P., was talking about his golf handicap. Six at Cypress Point, paired with Doug Sanders in the pro-am at the 1969 Crosby. Osmosis was not working, his sensors were not picking up my confession; there was no spiritual help coming from that quarter, only information on how to play the dogleg sixteenth at Pebble Beach. It was useless to try to explain to Jackie Kasey why I was so hesitant. Sure, I'm sure she gives great head, Jackie, but she never heard of Commando Kelly, no, he's different from Colin Kelly, it's just hard to explain why it's important to me. And so in the end I agreed to take out Teddi.

I called my wife in Los Angeles. She said that she was lonely and depressed. The septic tank had overflowed. There was a crash pad next door and one of the couples had taken to boffing on the grass in clear view of our daughter's bedroom window. The wind was blowing and there were fires at Point Dume. The maid had quit, the fire insurance had been canceled and the engine in the Corvette had seized on the Ventura Freeway. The Chevrolet agency refused to honor the warranty on the Corvette and so she had called Detroit and told the head of public relations at General Motors that

if the warranty was not honored she was going to drive
the car to Detroit and burn the motherfucker on the
lawn of John Z. DeLorean, vice-president and general
manager of the Chevrolet division of General motors.
The head of public relations had suggested she see a
psychiatrist. "What's new with you?" she said.

"Jackie's got me a date with a nineteen-year-old
tonight. She's supposed to suck me and fuck me."

"It's research," she said. "It's a type, the girl
who's always available to fuck the comic's friend.
You're missing the story if you don't meet her."

"But I don't *want* to fuck her."

There was a long silence at the other end of the
telephone. "Well, that can be part of the story, too," she
said.

There seemed nothing more to say. I was the one
who was supposed to be detached.

I placed another call to Los Angeles, to a forty-
four-year-old friend who lived in a swinging singles
complex in Marina del Rey. He had been married twice
for a grand total of eleven months and now had decided
to spend the rest of his years banging airline steward-
esses. He had, he said, a little money, no ambition and
plenty of seed. Two weeks before, he had visited me in
Las Vegas and said he was having a nervous collapse.
"There's a vise around my head," he had said.

"Thin," I said.

"Right."

"Seamless."

"Right."

"A steel band that gets tighter and tighter."

"Right."

He said he wanted to get laid. By a hooker. I

decided to keep him away from Artha. It might have
complicated our relationship. I found another cruising
the parking lot at the Dunes in a sea-green 1963 Oldsmobile 88. She wanted a hundred dollars. I said it was
not for me, it was for my friend, he was from out of
town, he wrote for *The Nation* and *The Nation* did not
pay much. She said the Oldsmobile had 93,000 miles on
it. Ninety-three thousand four hundred twelve point
eight, to be exact. She came down to seventy dollars,
then fifty. Her name was Sherry. She was from Miami.
She said things were tough in Vegas. I said things were
tough at *The Nation*. She did not read *The Nation*. We
settled on thirty dollars. I felt like John Alden. A
Nevada version. I went back to my own car.

"What does she look like?"

"You remember those Jewish girls we used to
bang in the Village back in the fifties? Who read Salin-
ger and went to the New School at night and listened
to Alfred Kazin lectures? She looked like that."

He put his hands over his eyes. I knew the vise
was tightening. He said, "Tell her I've already fucked
her."

I went back and told Sherry. She said she understood.

And now he was back in Marina del Rey seeking
the perfect stewardess. He could not comprehend why
nineteen was a problem.

"Does Teddi end with an *i* or an *ie?*" It was all
he wanted to know.

"I don't know."

"Find out."

"Is it important?" He seemed to have cracked a

sexual cipher of vowels and consonants and diphthongs that I could not begin to understand.

"You don't know how important," he said.

Teddi ended with an *i.* She had thick legs and called her mother "Bev." Bev had thrown her out of the house three months before. "I used to call her 'Mother,' " Teddi said. "It drove her crazy. She wanted to pretend we were sisters. Like when we double-dated."

"That makes sense," I said.

"She didn't want her dates to know she had a seventeen-year-old daughter," Teddi said.

"Oh, oh, you just made a boo-boo," Sandye said. Sandye was the keno runner at the Taj Mahal who was Jackie Kasey's girl friend and Teddi's roommate. She had cat's eyes that never seemed to focus directly and her face was heavily made up to cover the pockmarks. She was born on a farm in Oklahoma and brought up on another in Florida. There was an aura of failed Okie cunning about her that I liked.

"What boo-boo?" Jackie Kasey said. I had the feeling already that double-dating was not his métier, that he wished he had never pledged himself to get me sucked and fucked.

"Teddi claims she's nineteen," Sandye said.

"Not for everybody," Teddi said. "Just for John."

I did not want to know why. I asked for a drink. All they had in the apartment was crème de menthe and half a bottle of Curaçao.

"I could make you a crème de menthe frappé," Teddi said. "We have this blender, you see."

"Oh," I said desperately. "A Waring?"

"What?"

"I meant, what kind?"

"We got it with Blue Chip stamps."

"That's smart."

"What's smart."

"Making use of your Blue Chip stamps that way."

"Why?"

"Well, I know a lot of people who throw them away. Just rip them up and get rid of them."

"Gee, they could get a blender."

"I never thought of that."

It did not seem a promising start. Jackie and Sandye had taken over most of the couch and were necking ostentatiously. I moved onto a bar stool and concentrated on Teddi making the frappé. I could not think of anything I wanted less than a crème de menthe frappé.

"I've seen every picture Laurence Olivier ever made," Teddi said. She gave me the frappé and as an afterthought a napkin. There was an implication that Sir Laurence and I were of the same generation. "Did you see him in *Bunny Lake Is Missing?*"

"No, but I know Otto Preminger." It just slipped out. I had an insane feeling that the naming of a few famous people would bridge the years. Mike Nichols, Buck Henry, Dory Previn—phantom friendships were cemented in Teddi's living room. I scoured my mind for movie gossip, who was queer, who a lesbian, who sniffed cocaine, who mainlined smack.

"I want to be a great actress," Teddi said. "Ophelia, Lady Macbeth, Mrs. Goforth."

Jackie and Sandye came up for air. "Who the fuck is Mrs. Goforth?" Jackie Kasey said.

"In *The Milk Train Doesn't Stop Here Any More,*" Teddi said deliberately. "By Mr. Tennessee Williams."

"A hard part," I said. A dribble of crème de menthe frappé was easing down my chin and I searched for it as delicately as possible with my tongue. "An underappreciated play."

"No shit," Jackie Kasey said.

"No shit," I said, more belligerently than I intended. I had never seen *Milk Train,* let alone read it, and did not have a clue whether it was underappreciated or not. All I knew was that I was pushing forty and trying to keep a conversation going with a demented teen who thought she could play the Tallulah Bankhead part. I wondered what I had done wrong to get stuck with Teddi and not her mother Bev. Bev I could understand.

"Jackie, how goes it, buddy?" Danny Davis said.

"Great, Danny, great, really good business," Jackie Kasey said. We were under the marquee at the Riviera but he did not move to shake hands with Danny Davis or to introduce Teddi and Sandye. "Tom Jones was by the other night. How goes it with you?"

"Great, buddy, really great," Danny Davis said. He was a comic warming up for a singer named Vikki Carr in the big room at the Riviera. "Turning them away. Bill Cosby came by last night."

"Yeah, well, Cos is coming by my show tomorrow night," Jackie Kasey said. "Table for twelve."

"I took a little steam with Alan King this afternoon," Danny Davis said. "See you around, buddy."

•   •   •

Jackie Kasey took a quarter from Sandye and
pumped it into a slot machine. "Alan King doesn't even
get into town until tomorrow," he said bitterly.

That Tom Jones had not stopped by was beside
the point. That Bill Cosby did not have a table for
twelve the next night was also beside the point. The
point was not to get topped by Danny Davis. The point
was that he should have been able to come up with a
superstar he had taken some steam with. Woody Allen,
Jack Carter, Jack E. Leonard, Frank Gorshin. That was
the point and he had blown it.

"Hey, let's go," Jackie Kasey said. He was im-
patient and it was time to get into the lounge. See Jan
Murray's second show and forget about Danny Davis.
Just remember always have someone's name on the tip
of your tongue you just took some steam with. Or
played a little handball with. Johnny Unitas. That was
even better than Jack Carter. Mickey Mantle. So anyone can take some steam with Alan King. Mickey Mantle, that's a different story. *Mick was telling me about
the time he belted number five hundred, five double-0.*
Jackie Kasey began to feel better. "Shake it, Sandye,
shake it."

The captain who brought us to our table cased
Sandye appraisingly. "Hey, you're coming up in the
world," he said. "Going out with headliners. I remember when you was just a broken-down keno runner at
the Taj."

"Yeah, well, I'm still just a broken-down keno
runner at the Taj," Sandye said.

The captain nodded wisely. "Sure you are."

"Fuck you," Sandye said.

The headwaiter got under her skin. At least it

gave us something to talk about. What was wrong with being a keno runner, what was so broken-down about that? The nerve of some people. Show me a headwaiter and I'll show you a pimp. At least in Vegas. Everyone knows that.

"How old are you?" someone in the audience asked Jan Murray.

"I am fifty-three years of age," Jan Murray said.

"What kind of Jewish name is Jan Murray?" someone else said.

"My real name is Murray Janofsky."

"Thirty-five years he's been telling people his name is Murray Janofsky," Jackie Kasey said. "Look at the clientele in here. Ninety percent Jewish. They come to hear him say his name used to be Murray Janofsky. Big deal."

"I'd rather be a broken-down keno runner than a pimp, that's for sure," Sandye said.

They were at cross-purposes. That left Teddi and me. She toyed with her orange juice. I wondered if she had a distorted cervix or had ever cried in a taxicab. It did not seem the time to ask.

"I collect swizzle sticks," Teddi said. "Some people collect matchbooks, I collect swizzle sticks."

"So did Ernest Hemingway," I said. It just popped into my head. "He was a famous swizzle-stick collector. One of the best. Harry's Bar, places like that. Cuba, Key West, you know, places like that. If they had swizzle sticks, he collected them. No doubt about that, none at all. He was famous for it."

"You got a real gift for small talk, John," Jackie Kasey said.

I was in too deep to give it up. "He was unspeak-

able about Scott Fitzgerald," I said. "Kept on talking
about the size of his dick."

The tempo picked up. The male organ, even of
a dead novelist three of the four people at the table had
never heard of, was something we could all relate to. It
was better stuff than whether the headwaiter was a
pimp, it beat complaining about Murray Janofsky. We
wondered how big it really was. About the size of a
swizzle stick. I tried not to visualize Scott Fitzgerald's
member with the words "Entertainment Capital of the
World" printed on it.

"Out of sight," Sandye said.

"Fantastic," Teddi said.

"Weird," Jackie Kasey said.

"You ever read *Gatsby?*" I said.

The spell was broken.

"It's past my bedtime," Teddi said.

"It's early," I said. "By my watch. Have I
shown you this watch? I bought it in Switzerland. Only
seventy-two Swiss francs. That's eighteen dollars
American. I've had it for ten years. Never given me any
trouble at all. I just don't believe in buying expensive
watches."

"You're a regular Murray Janofsky, John,"
Jackie Kasey said.

"I've got a dance class at eight o'clock," Teddi
said. "Classical ballet. I don't approve of modern
dance."

"I can agree with that." '

We drove home in silence. She lived behind the
Tropicana, in a block of units distinguished only by
their sameness. I walked her to the door. "Can I call
you?"

"I'm in the book."

"I didn't catch your last name."

"Sandye has it."

I moved to kiss her, but as I did she turned to put the key into the latch. My lips landed hard on the back of her fall. It fell on the "Welcome" mat. She picked it up and blocked the doorway.

"I'll see you around," I said.

"I work nights," Teddi said. She closed the door.

"We still got to get him laid," Jackie Kasey said. It was later and we were sitting in the Crown Room at the top of the International. He seemed chagrined that the evening with Teddi was less than a success. The thought of coupling with a teenager whose given name ended in *i* filled me with a low dread, even more so than it had at the beginning of the evening.

"He's married, it doesn't matter," Sandye said.

"Sure, it matters, he's been away from home for a long time, he's frustrated, he wants to get his ashes hauled," Jackie Kasey said.

They talked as if I were not present. I felt like a bolt of cloth in a draper's window, two yards of freight salvage being pinched for value.

"Carla Moran."

"She's got hair on her tits."

"How do you know?"

"I know."

"She's got a kid anyway."

"And he doesn't want to get involved," Jackie Kasey said. "You want to get involved?"

I had a role to play. "In free, out free," I said.

"I only been involved a couple of times," Jackie Kasey said. He waved his hand in the general direction of Sandye. Now it was she who seemed not to be present. "Something like this chick, well, you know what I mean."

"I like a good time," Sandye said. Sweet acned Sandye. "You have a good time and then you get married. There's a lot of opportunities in Vegas. People always like to gamble."

I wondered what that had to do with getting married.

"You find a pit boss, he's never out of work," Sandye said. "A good pit boss is hard to find, they're always at a premium."

"Bonnie Decter," Jackie Kasey said.

"She got busted," Sandye said. "Shoplifting."

"Maybe we just ought to take him to the Pussycat," Jackie Kasey said. The Pussycat was a club on the Strip where the local people went in the pre-dawn hours. Rock music, three deep at the bar, a pickup place. I had the feeling that Jackie Kasey was tiring of the charade, and also of Sandye. There had been too many keno runners and maybe he did not want to wake up alongside another. The Pussycat must have seemed the perfect place to unload the both of us.

"There's a lot of heads there," Sandye said. "If you'll excuse the expression."

"He knows what heads are," Jackie Kasey muttered.

"I mean," Sandye said, "I didn't know if he was cool."

It was nearly four in the morning and I found myself trying to ratify my coolness, asking where one *scored* in Vegas, how much a *lid* was, and was the *Man* as *heavy* as I heard, was it true you could get ten years for *dealing.*

"I didn't know you were so cool," Sandye said. Jackie was also appraising me in a new light, as if right there in the Crown Room he had found someone on whom he could unload his keno runner.

"I think maybe I'll just hit the sack," I said.

"I mean, you are really cool," Sandye said.

Cooler than a pit boss, I wondered.

"Linda Kirby," Jackie Kasey said. "I'll call her. Tell her to suck and fuck you."

He never did. For which I was grateful.

TWELVE

Buster Mano fileted a Hostess Twinkie as neatly as if it were a Dover sole. With a butter knife he scooped the cream filling from each half of the cupcake, leaving a hollow in each like a pitted avocado. Buster never ate the cream in a Twinkie; he claimed the filling made him bind up. His lower intestine was a Dunkirk always waiting to be evacuated and Buster kept up-to-the-minute status reports on the departure readiness of his bowels. He signaled the waitress for a half cup of coffee. Hot and weak. The waitress extracted a pencil from the northern extremities of her lavender-tinted beehive and pondered the order. A half cup, hot and weak. "I don't know about that," she said. The plastic name tag on her uniform identified her as "Reeta" and her lavender hairdo was peaked with a tiny white hat on which was printed, DENNY'S—OPEN 24-HRS.—A VEGAS LAND-MARK SINCE 1966.

"Know about what?" Buster Mano said.

"We don't serve half cups at Denny's."

"A whole cup tends to get cold before you finish," Buster Mano said.

"I'd have to charge you for a full cup," Reeta persisted.

"The menu says all the coffee you can drink for the price of a cup," Buster Mano said. "So it doesn't matter if the first cup's a whole cup or a half cup, does it?"

"I guess I never really thought of it that way," Reeta said.

"Takes thinking," Buster Mano said. "A half cup, then."

Reeta studied her order pad. "You wouldn't mind if I wrote down a full cup on the check and not a half cup, would you?" she said. "The boss might think it's funny, you know, ordering a half cup."

"Sure thing."

"You're nice. You from Vegas?"

Buster shook his head and mentioned the name of a Midwestern city.

"The nice ones never come from Vegas," Reeta said. "I'm from Fresno, and believe me, have I got a story."

"I bet," Buster Mano said, not unkindly. "The coffee."

"Half cup coming up," Reeta said.

Buster quartered his Twinkie and dunked a quadrant into the half cup of coffee. He closed his eyes as he ate, smiling to himself, and then finally he said, eyes still shut, "Harold Pugh."

I did not realize I was supposed to reply.

Buster opened his eyes and dabbed a piece of Twinkie from his lips. "Harold Pugh," he repeated.

I took the bait. "Who is Harold Pugh?"

Buster Mano smiled. "Harold Pugh," he said, "is a loser."

•   •   •

A casino downtown had asked Buster Mano to locate Harold Pugh. It was a small matter. Harold Pugh had run out on a marker of $2,700 and dropped out of sight. His telephone had been disconnected and a hooker named Moreen was now living in his apartment. Moreen had never heard of Harold Pugh. Moreen said she had put two months' rent down on the apartment and to leave her the fuck alone. She had juice, she had a boy friend who had eight points in the Thunderbird and her boy friend had connections downtown and his connections would lean on anyone who bothered her. Who the fuck was Harold Pugh anyway? A nobody.

Moreen was right. Harold Pugh was a nobody and the casino decided to let matters drop. Gambling debts are legally uncollectable and $2,700 was not enough to get upset over. Better to eat $2,700, especially when it might cost two bills to find Harold Pugh. Nor was $2,700 worth any rough stuff. Not that Harold Pugh's disappearance did not rankle. Money was money, there was a principle involved. It was just that it was hard to think of Harold Pugh in terms of principle. He was a steady player, a good player, he knew the layout and figured the percentages. A quiet little fellow from Fort Smith, Arkansas. The only thing that anyone could really remember about him was that he hated the niggers. His daughter had drowned in an integrated community swimming pool in Fort Smith and Harold Pugh blamed Martin Luther King. It was a stretch, but everything about Harold Pugh was a stretch. He came to Vegas after his daughter died and got a job selling dice. Dice and the Reverend M. L. King were the only two things Harold Pugh ever talked about. Always M. L. King, never Martin Luther King. He liked to hold a pair of dice in his hand and talk about the tolerances. Precision-milled to one ten-thousandth of an inch. Sand-finished rather than clear, because the added friction gave dice more action on the table. He would stand at a crap table at three o'clock in the morning and talk about dice. He always gambled downtown. There were too many Jews on the Strip. Jews and M. L. King, there was the trouble with the world. A pair of dice was the only thing that had any meaning. Harold Pugh claimed to sell eight thousand pairs of dice a month, $1.40 a pair. It was a good living, he had no major expenses. Just a girl friend, a dim number with no tits who had flunked the dealer's test at a gambling school. The blackjack test, the easiest one to learn. A typical Harold Pugh girl friend. The girl friend never went gambling with Harold Pugh. He would always stand at the table alone and go into his monologue about dice. Never to anyone in particular. Just to himself. If anyone was listening, fine. It was for this reason that there was never much action at any table where Harold Pugh was playing. The voice was quiet, obsessive. Dice, the only thing in the world that has any meaning. Three quarters of an inch to a side, edges razor-sharp, made from cellulose nitrate, you call it celluloid, heaviest of all the thermoplastics, the spots are flush, that's because recessed spots make the six side too light, I bet you didn't know the heat from your hand distorts the tolerance, thirty days, that's as long as you should keep dice on the shelf, after that give them to the USO. Harold Pugh was a nut about dice as he was about M. L. King.

It was a pit boss from the casino downtown who spotted Harold Pugh coming out of the Valley Bank of Nevada branch in Henderson. The pit boss had often

talked to Harold Pugh about dice and he knew there
was a $2,700 marker and that Harold had quit his job
and left town four months before. Or so everyone had
surmised. The pit boss told his shift boss that he had
seen Harold Pugh in Henderson and the shift manager
told the casino manager and the casino manager called
Buster Mano. It was not the sort of case that Buster
Mano usually took on, but he was offered not only his
time but five percent of the marker. Buster said ten
percent or find another boy. Seven and a half, the casino
manager said. Ten, Buster Mano repeated. It was a
matter of some honor with him. It was Buster's considered opinion that the People controlled all the casinos
and when dealing with the People the only way one
could salvage some dignity was to get top dollar. That
is the only language they understand, Buster would say.
Never mind that ten percent in this case is only $270,
it is still top dollar. And two seventy plus time is better
than a kick in the ass.

Buster Mano got his ten percent and immediately went to work. He sent a third-class letter to Harold Pugh's last known address, knowing that while the
post office would not forward third-class mail, it often
put a forwarding address on the letter before returning
it to the sender. The letter came back to Buster Mano
address unknown and he carefully noted on his expense
sheet, "One U.S. stamp—8¢." Next he checked his
I.B.M. printout of power-meter credits. The credit
printout was issued every month and covered the
preceding twelve-month period. Anyone who had
transferred his utilities over the past year was listed in
that book. Again no luck. Buster placed a call to the
casino manager. "What's the name of Harold Pugh's
girl friend?"

"The one with no tits?"

"She might have three tits for all I know."

"I'll get back to you."

The name of the girl with no tits was LaVerne. No known last name. She had once worked as a cocktail waitress at the Stardust. Buster called a friend in the security office of the Stardust. The friend said he would see what he could do. On his expense sheet Buster noted, "Two telephone calls—20¢."

The friend at the Stardust called back the next day. "LaVerne Burdette. A real dumbbell. No tits."

Buster checked the power company printout. Four months earlier LaVerne Burdette had moved from an apartment on Rome in Las Vegas to another in Henderson. Her new telephone number was 456–2033. Buster dialed the number.

"Hello."

"LaVerne Burdette?" Buster's voice was up half an octave, quick, exhilarated.

"Yes."

"Les Lacy, LaVerne, KENO Radio, the sound of Las Vegas for over twenty-eight years."

"Yes."

"How about that, LaVerne, I bet you're not even twenty-eight yourself. You sound like a . . . twenty-four."

"I'm twenty-seven, Les."

"How about that? Married, LaVerne?"

"Not yet, Les."

"But a boy friend, though, right?"

"That's right."

"And what does that lucky young man do?"

"He's in sales."

"In sales! How about that? What does he sell?"

"Patio furniture."

"Patio furniture. How about that? It wouldn't be for White Front, would it. White Front is a sponsor, got to get in every plug we can, you understand that, I bet, LaVerne."

"I sure do, Les. He works for Mojave Lawn and Patio."

"Would you believe that's another sponsor, La-Verne."

"This is just so wonderful, Les."

"And it's going to be even more wonderful, La-Verne. Now, listen, you've heard my show . . ."

"Oh, sure, Les."

"Well, you know we give away albums, La-Verne, if you can answer the lucky question."

"I never win anything, Les."

"Your luck is going to change right here, La-Verne. Ready or not, here it comes."

"I'm so scared."

"It's a tough one, LaVerne. Now, for the original sound-track album of *The Sound of Music,* I want you to tell me who was the star of the movie version of that hit Broadway musical."

"Julie . . . Andrews."

"LaVerne, I thought you told me you never win anything, but you have just won an original sound-track album of *The Sound of Music* with Julie Andrews and all those other great stars. Isn't that exciting?"

"Oh, boy, Les. Listen, there's just one thing. I've already got Julie on *The Sound of Music.*"

"LaVerne, sweetie, now you've got two. Let me ask you something. You got a mom?"

"Sure do, Les."

"Well, now with your new album you've got

your mom her Christmas present next December. A little early Christmas shopping, LaVerne, isn't that exciting?"

"It sure is, Les."

"*Ciao*, LaVerne, it's been great talking to you."

Buster Mano hung up the telephone. His brow was beaded with sweat. A long low fart whistled through his office.

"Jesus, I thought I was going to cut one when I was talking to her," Buster Mano said. "It would have blown the whole number. Maybe I blew it anyway. I should have told her the show was on tape. She's probably twisting the dials right now trying to find me." He farted again. "Oh, well, you live and learn," Buster Mano said.

"Why?" I asked.

"Why what?" Buster Mano said.

"Why do you do it?"

"You mean, what's my motivation?"

"Yes."

"You asshole."

It was the next morning and Buster Mano and I were driving to the casino downtown with the information about Harold Pugh. Buster had called the Mojave Lawn and Patio and they had volunteered that Harold Pugh would that afternoon be setting up a patio display in a model home in a subdivision called Rio del Sol.

"Polished terrazzo benches?" Buster Mano had asked.

"Oh, absolutely. Stain-resistant to any food and drink."

"Just what I'm looking for," Buster Mano had said.

There was a tape recorder beside me on the front seat of the car and the cassette was monitoring our conversation. Buster hefted the tape recorder in his hand.

"I'm trying to find Harold Pugh, you're trying to find me, there's no difference. You're the same kind of Peeping Tom I am. Except I don't give a shit. I like looking for people and I cleared eighteen grand last year before taxes. So don't give me that crap about motivation. Motivation is a very poor explanation of character."

I shut off the tape recorder.

"No dramatic gestures," Buster Mano said. He switched the machine back on. "By the way, did you fuck that spade who was in your apartment that night?"

We parked the car and went into the casino. Buster never gambled, but he knew a number of the players at the tables. Buster preferred downtown to the Strip. It was a city and he understood cities. Cities meant failure and he was a connoisseur of failure.

"Buster."

"How are you?"

"Jack Eastern, Buster."

"I'd know you anywhere, Jack."

"What's it been, Buster?"

"Three years anyway, Jack. You're looking good."

"Fuck looking good, Buster. I'm seventy-four years old."

"Never would have figured that, Jack."

"Stopped playing golf four years ago."

"What are you doing for exercise?"

"I'd walk up Fremont Street buck ass naked if I could stop getting old."

"I'd like to take you up on that, Jack."

"Only thing worse than dying is getting old."

"That's a grim son of a bitch thought," Buster Mano said.

The casino manager was pleased at the progress of Buster Mano's investigation. He sat in his Naugahyde desk chair, a heavy-set man with a wall eye, and twirled the dial of a closed-circuit television set on the desk in front of him. Each channel zeroed in on a different pit. He was watching a blackjack game. "Look at that losing son of a bitch," he said. "He'll hit an eighteen, you watch."

The player took a queen. The dealer paid eighteen.

The manager turned off the set. "With stiffs like him, this could be a good business," he said. He was wearing a white-on-white shirt with his initials monogrammed on the cuffs. It was hard to tell which was his good eye, whether he was looking at Buster or me. "So you found Harold."

Buster Mano grunted. "What do you want me to do?"

"Get the money back."

"How bad you want it?"

"We'll settle. Even like his business back. Cash business."

"And if he won't settle?"

"That son of a bitch likes to gamble too much. I'll put his picture in every casino in town."

"You got his picture?"

"You got a Polaroid?"
"Gotcha."

The Rio del Sol subdivision was off Flamingo Road east of the Strip. Pastel ranch styles, terrazzo roofs, two-car garages. There was a developer's sign in front of the model house—OPEN FOR INSPECTION— LOW DOWN—VHA/FHA—FROM $22,995.

Buster Mano walked through the living room with his Polaroid camera in hand. "You don't mind if I take pictures?" he asked the real-estate agent. "For the little woman. She works days at the Sands."

"Really," the real-estate woman said. She was a hefty blonde, nearing sixty, in a miniskirt, and her voice was guarded, as if LOW DOWN—VHA/FHA—FROM $22,995 was too steep for the husband of what she seemed to assume was a cocktail waitress at the Sands.

Buster Mano caught the hesitation. "In the publicity department," he said.

"Of course, go right ahead," the real-estate woman said.

Buster Mano began snapping pictures with his Polaroid.

"You'll notice the light dimmer," the real-estate agent said.

"I like the push-button controls," Buster Mano said.

"And it's all name-brand furniture. Of course it doesn't come with every house, but the manufacturer is willing to give a discount. And no separate financing. It would all come with the initial loan."

"With approval of credit, I presume." Buster Mano smiled.

"Oh, of course. And isn't the breakfast nook darling? An all-electric kitchen."

"We have butane now," Buster Mano said. "The wife hates it."

"Well, then, this is the place for you."

Buster Mano tore off a snapshot, nodded with satisfaction and put the photograph in his pocket. "It's the patio I'm really interested in," he said. "We spend all our time on the patio. Ruth and the dog and myself. We don't have any children. Mustard, our dog, he's family enough for us."

"That's delightful."

We went out the sliding glass door to the patio. Harold Pugh was arranging a rattan grouping around the barbecue. On a rattan cocktail table there was a tray full of empty plastic liquor bottles, a Scotch-plaid ice bucket and some tinted plastic patio glasses.

"I'd just love a picture of that," Buster Mano said. He motioned Harold Pugh to one of the rattan chairs. "Could you sit in a chair? I want my Ruth to get the full flavor of it."

Harold Pugh moved reluctantly into the chair. He was a small ferret-faced man in a dark suit and a string tie. On his right pinky finger was a diamond ring with the stones worked into the initials "H.P."

Buster Mano raised the camera to his eye. "It's a wonderful effect with the bottles," he said. "A real selling point. Just like home."

The real-estate woman came out onto the patio. "I didn't give you my card. I'm Mrs. Becker. And this is Mr. Pugh from Mojave Lawn and Patio. I can't wait for your wife . . ."

"Ruth."

"Of course, Ruth, I can't wait for Ruth to see the patio."

"Do you have any other kind of patio suites?" Buster Mano said. He tore off the snapshot and showed it to Harold Pugh. "You should smile more," Buster Mano said.

"Contemporary or classic?" Harold Pugh said.

"Polished terrazzo," Buster Mano said.

"We'd have to order it," Harold Pugh said. "Six-week delivery."

"I'm afraid you'd skip town if we gave you six weeks, Harold," Buster Mano said.

Harold Pugh sat transfixed in the rattan chair. His bones seemed to have collapsed. He tried to wipe his forehead, but he could barely lift his arm.

"I'm sure Mr. Pugh could have it here quicker than six weeks," Mrs. Becker said.

"Five weeks, I could write you an order," Harold Pugh said weakly.

"Oh, shit, Harold," Buster Mano said. He looked at the snapshot once again. "You take such a good picture."

"I'm sure I don't understand," Mrs. Becker said.

"Tell her, Harold," Buster Mano said.

Harold Pugh tried to rise from the chair. "That stupid LaVerne," he said finally. "You know that dumb bitch really thought she was going to get *The Sound of Music.*"

Buster Mano extended a hand to help Harold Pugh from the chair. "Oh, hell, I'll buy her the album, Harold," Buster Mano said.

2

For a while I neither called Buster Mano nor returned his calls. In fact I was not seeing anyone again. The whole Harold Pugh episode had vitiated my desire for human contact. I wanted to be left alone as I wished I had left Harold Pugh alone. Not that it would have made any difference. It was just that I felt like an accomplice in a mugging. What did it have to do with me? Why was I there? What life lesson had I learned?

This capacity for voyeurism was like a virus lodged in my upper respiratory system. I could pinpoint with computer accuracy the first attack. It was at a time in my life—I was in my middle twenties—when I was particularly susceptible. I lived in New York and led an almost completely vicarious existence. I had taken to greeting people with the word "Howdy," which as greetings go is not bad, peculiar in fact only when emerging from the lips of an Irish Catholic from Hartford, Connecticut. I had a job I hated and was picking up the pieces after behaving badly with a rich and well-connected girl I never had any intention of marrying. She was a devout Catholic and retailed every sexual spasm to her confessor. I would watch her go into the confessional box at St. Patrick's Cathedral, a black mantilla on her hair, rosary beads coiled in her fingers, and when she emerged her relief was visible. Hours later in bed, a sinner again, she would say a perfect Act of Contrition before going to sleep so that if death came in the night it would find her cleansed of mortal sin. Her family was vaguely theatrical and I was stage-struck; I hoped to make use of the connections to get into the theater. It was the way I thought things were accomplished in those days. But I had neither the talent, nor perhaps even the heart, for this kind of manipulation. A few more fevered couplings, a few more fervent Acts of Contrition, and then the affair was over. (She entered a convent, became a feminist, married a priest; she helped draft evaders flee to Canada and is now living and rolfing in a commune in Saskatchewan. We correspond fitfully.)

Most of my acquaintances belonged to this affair and out of mutual embarrassment we stopped seeing each other. There was no one I wished to see, only those I wished to know. I would walk home from work in the late spring light, never the same way two nights running, and I would go into funeral homes on the East Side to see if anyone famous had died. I would sign the book, shake hands with the widow and tell her how much I had enjoyed her husband's music or fiction or work on the stage. Thank you, she would murmur, you are so kind. Other nights I would walk into brownstones and check the mailboxes to see if I recognized any of the names. I knew where Henry Fonda lived and John Steinbeck and Harold S. Prince and Tammy Grimes. And I knew that an aging *grande dame* of the Broadway theater was living with the juvenile lead of their foundering comedy, knew because I had seen his name scrawled in pencil under hers on the Tiffany calling card that identified her mailbox in a Turtle Bay town house. I did not know what I expected to do with this information, but it was mine and I cached it in the pigeonholes of my mind like a child hoarding agates.

To shake this lassitude, I changed apartments and moved into a block of flats on East 84th Street that had been built in the late thirties as a monument to the idea of gracious living on a middle income. My building exactly duplicated the one across the street, which was owned and operated by the same real-estate complex; each individual apartment corresponded in every detail to the one across the street, from the number of the flat to the location of the lighting fixtures. I lived on the north side of 84th Street in apartment 4-C, and because of the configuration of the street, I could look slightly down and directly into apartment 4-C across the way. Except for the furniture it was a perfect copy of my flat even to the decorative nonfunctioning fireplace adorning the far living-room wall.

The day I moved into my new apartment I was introduced, in a manner of speaking, to the routine of the tenant in 4-C across the street. She was a large, good-looking woman of perhaps thirty, very tall, nearly six feet, long blond hair, well-proportioned figure. She came home from work that afternoon, and as she would every afternoon, opened the window, turned the stereo on loud, made herself a drink, took off her clothes and then stark-naked, using her drink as a baton, began to conduct Mozart's Concerto #5 in A-Major.

I never knew her name nor made any effort to find out. I stopped investigating mailboxes and funeral homes. She required total concentration. I sat in a chair by the window of my darkened apartment, like a field artillery forward observer searching for a fire mission. If I was a voyeur, however, she was an exhibitionist. Her shades were never drawn, her lights never dimmed. Her life was a book whose pages I felt free to turn. I tended to linger over the erotic passages. She fucked constantly. It was the first time I recall most vividly. I had been to see a movie and when I came home the

lights were on in her apartment and the shades up and
her legs were wrapped around the back of a man who
was driving in and out of her as monotonously as a
metronome. I had never watched anyone fuck before.
It was oddly compelling and oddly unstimulating, for
the viewer from across the street a mechanical problem
having more to do with movement, friction and lubrica-
tion than sexual pleasure, something like watching a
slide lecture on the workings of a Bessemer converter.

I watched until they were finished and then went
to bed. The event had as little impact on me as the first
time I had seen Raymond E. Baldwin, governor of
Connecticut. The next morning, as I was shaving, I
could see the girl's lover standing in her bedroom drinking a cup of coffee. The face seemed familiar. He came
closer to the window. He had been a classmate of mine
at Princeton.

I had never much liked him. In my Senior Class
Poll, he had received ninety-seven votes in the category
"Most Respected." He married a girl from Smith with
automotive money and a weight problem. They moved
to New York and progressed from Stuyvesant Town to
Murray Hill to a co-op on the Spanish Harlem side of
96th and Park. That day I called him at the advertising
agency where he worked and asked him to lunch. We
talked about a lot of things, about people we knew and
what they were doing, who was divorced and who had
died, who was working for Proctor & Gamble and who
for Young & Rubicam. I asked about his wife. She was
visiting her family. His daughter? On the waiting list at
Brearley. The waiting list? Schools are harder to get
into these days.

By the second drink we had exhausted every-

thing we had to say to each other and finally I said that
I had heard his family was out of town and had called
the night before about dinner. I said that there had been
no answer at his apartment. He said he had gone to a
movie by himself, come home, watched television and
gone to bed.

A good movie?

A John Wayne picture on 86th Street.

The RKO?

I don't really remember.

I told him that I had not realized the Wayne
picture was playing the nabes. I thought it was still
first-run on Broadway.

He picked at his London broil and said nothing.
I knew his agency had just lost the account he was
working on and that he was afraid of losing his job and
that while his family was out of town he was pounding
it home to a girl who conducted Mozart in the nude
with a tumbler of J&B Scotch as a baton. I knew and
for some reason I thought I had a kind of moral advan-
tage over him.

He only came to apartment 4-C once. Not that
she lacked companionship. There was the man who in
a moment of careless rapture tried to pick her up and
bring her to bed, only to stumble as he underestimated
her size and drop her on the floor. There was the man
who, equally naked as she, played a flute solo during
her rendition of the Concerto #5 in A-Major. And
there was the man who never even loosened his tie while
she went down on him on the living-room couch. I
knew them all, and yet all the while I tried to formulate
ground rules about the girl in 4-C. I would not watch
her obsessively, but failed to define "obsessively." I was

James Stewart in *Rear Window,* a Hitchcock hero and
not a dirty old man. I was a voyeur and not a Peeping
Tom (the one seemed less pathological and clinical than
the other).

Whatever I was, there developed between us a
kind of symbiosis. Over the next couple of years I would
see her on buses, I would sit next to her at the theater,
I would look up in a restaurant and she would be staring at me. There was never a flicker of recognition, but
each of us was perfectly aware of the other. It was as
if we were caught in some kind of extrasensory entan-
glement comforting to us both. With the passage of
time and an upswing in my own life, I rarely watched
her sexual performances. But in an odd way she was
family and I knew all her little household behavior
patterns as well as an FBI stakeout knows the personal
habits of a Mafia don. I knew that she changed her
sheets on Wednesday and watered the plants on Friday
and picked up the laundry on Monday, that she always
put a raw egg in her orange juice at breakfast and that
she never left the apartment without turning off all the
lights. She might leave every light on when she was
fucking, but not even the hall light was lit when she
went out.

It was the lights that caught my attention. I
became aware without thinking much about it that they
had been on for several days. On when I went to work
in the morning, on when I came home at night, on when
I rose in the middle of the night to go to the bathroom.
On, and yet there seemed to be no one in the apartment.
I tried to remember the last time I had seen her. It had
been some time since I had watched, but I had always
been aware of a presence in 4-C across 84th Street,

aware that the stereo was on or that the flowers had been changed or that there was someone cooking in the kitchen. Now the flowers were wilted and there was no Mozart. They were cut flowers, white roses in a glass vase, and the petals began to brown and drop. Five days, six, a week passed. I had known this girl from afar for nearly three years, better perhaps than the men who had passed through her apartment, and now she had vanished. Night after night I would sit in front of my window and stare across at her vacant apartment. A vacation? She would have turned out the lights, she would have made the bed, she would have thrown out the flowers, she was compulsively neat. That her apartment was an exact duplicate of mine became a factor in my obsession. There were four bulbs in the living-room fixture, three in the bedroom, two each in the kitchen and hallway. One by one the bulbs began to burn out. Hour by hour I would wait for a filament to blaze brightly before going dark. I began to imagine the worst accidents, the direst crimes. Murder, accident, suicide. There was a man who had beaten her up one night, a year or so before. I tried to remember what he looked like, tall, short, light, dark, fat, thin. Had he really beaten her up or were they cuffing each other playfully like cub bears? A filament flashed, another bulb went out.

I told no one except the girl I was later to marry. She came back to my apartment with me one night and we sat and stared, neither of us saying a word, until exhaustion finally took us to bed with each other for the first time. The next morning she insisted that I tell the superintendent of my building, who was also the super for the building across the street. I began to waffle. Tell him what? That some chick's lights have been on for ten days?

That she might have been murdered. That she might have fallen in the bathtub and fractured her skull. That she might have taken an overdose.

Of what?

Don't be obtuse.

I was finally less persuaded than shamed into going down to the super's apartment in the basement. I stood outside and raised my hand to knock at his door. Then I stopped. Wait a minute, wait just a damn minute, let's think this through, let's consider all the permutations. What indeed if there had been violence? I could conjure up the scenario. The police investigating the crime. A logical cop question: who reported it. I imagined myself in a cubbyhole office at Manhattan North Homicide, a light shining in my face, barely able to make out the clutch of shadowy detectives throwing questions at me. How long had I been watching this girl? Why had I watched her? How had I gained entrance to her apartment? Where had I found the kitchen knife to stab her or the sash weight to bash her head? At best I would be found innocent, but branded on page three of the *Daily News* a Peeping Tom, not a Hitchcock hero, Jimmy Stewart was never a Peeping Tom. And so I fled the basement without knocking on the super's door.

Five bulbs left, three, two and then the apartment was in total darkness. Two weeks and two days had passed since I had first noticed that there was something strange going on across the street. I went to see the superintendent.

He was an odious man, a quality which I think

is a prerequisite for being a New York apartment superintendent. He had complained when I had painted a
room in my apartment orange and we had fought over
his refusal to fix a pipe leaking into my kitchen. I had
told him one winter to go fuck himself when he would
not turn up the heat in my apartment and I had not
tipped him for the preceding two Christmases. And
now here I was trying to sound casual, a possible acces-
sory to murder. Howdy, I said. I was an insomniac, I
said, and the lights in 4-C across the street had kept me
awake for several weeks now, I'm sure there's nothing
to it, I think there's a girl living there, I don't really pay
that much attention, maybe a married couple, but the
fact is they usually turn off their lights, at least during
the day, and these lights, you know, they've been burning out, and I thought, well, as you're the superintendent for both buildings, you might want to check, it's the
apartment directly across from mine, I guess it would
be the fourth floor, I don't check these things too
closely, I just want to be a good neighbor, I'd hate to
think there might have been an accident and I had not
reported it, it's the curse of living in New York, people
don't want to get involved and it's really a terrible
thing, not getting involved, I mean.

    The super listened to this insane chatter, his face
fathomless, and I wondered if I could make out two
retroactive Christmas checks to him. You know, it's
just come to my attention, I got a call from my business
manager and he said he could not find the last two
Christmas checks, he was sure he had sent them out, he
knew how important the super was to me, how much
I treasured all he had done for me, it must be the New
York mail, you can never trust the Post Office, they're

civil servants, they don't have the same desire to help
that an apartment superintendent has, please accept my
apologies and take two months' rent for the last two
Christmases, no, I insist, really insist.

The super said he would check out the apartment across the street, and that there was just one thing
he wanted to say.

I thought for sure it would be, Hold yourself
available for questioning.

The orange room in your apartment, he said.
When your lease is up, you got to paint it back white.
We don't pay for no orange room. You got to pay for
that yourself.

I did not tell him to fuck off.

The rest of the story is an anticlimax. The super
went across the street, the girl was not there, there was
no foul play, she had eloped and I never saw her again.
Never looked up and saw her ahead of me at the check-
out counter at D'Agostino's. Never saw her in the
queue at the Trans-Lux 85th Street. But the point I
discovered during those sessions by the window in
apartment 4-C was that I had a gift for voyeurism. I was
good at it, and imagined I had an empathy for those I
observed. I liked to think, I told myself then, and was
still telling myself that summer in Vegas, that I could
learn something about myself from the people whose
lives I intruded upon, indeed that this was the reason
I had taken up residence in an apartment behind the
Strip. Perhaps I even believed this. Perhaps it was even
true.

3

Harold Pugh arranged to pay off his marker at the casino downtown at the rate of fifty dollars a week from his salary plus commission at Mojave Lawn and Patio. Every couple of days a shift boss would call Harold to pass the time and to make sure he had not left town. Occasionally, late at night, Harold Pugh would come into the casino and play craps and talk about dice. Tolerances to one twentieth the thickness of human hair. Once had seventy active dice accounts, he would say, including one in Yugoslavia. Reason for the account in Yugoslavia was that Marshal Tito learned how to play craps from a P-38 Lightning pilot shot down during the Second World War. The one we won, Harold Pugh called it. Then one night Harold Pugh had a hot streak and won six hundred dollars. The next day he did not show up at the Mojave Lawn and Patio, and efforts to find him in Las Vegas were unavailing. Both the apartment and the telephone were in LaVerne Burdette's name, and she was left to pay both bills. She returned to work as a cocktail waitress at the Thunderbird and claimed that in the six months they were together Harold Pugh had fucked her only eight times. It was assumed that Harold Pugh had returned to Fort Smith, Arkansas.

PART

5

THIRTEEN

There was a telegram stuck in the bedroom mirror of Jackie Kasey's suite on the twenty-fifth floor of the hotel. "Coming from Philadelphia Thursday. Include me for dinner." It was signed "Brother Hugh." Jackie Kasey thought, Oh, shit, that's all I need. He jammed a menthol inhalator into his nose and stood there for a moment in the center of the room, hands on his hips, the inhalator hanging out of his nose like a piece of frozen extruded mucus. One hundred thirteen degrees outside and he had a cold, two weeks he had a cold. Steam, sauna, whirlpool, pills, capsules, medicine, two pokes of penicillin in the ass and one poke of vitamin B, nothing got rid of the goddam cold. Think positive, Jackie Kasey thought. Maybe the cold was a blessing. Maybe he would have a fever Thursday and then maybe he wouldn't have to go on and then maybe Hugh Hill would not see the shape the act was in. Not that the act was bad, nothing of the sort. He just wanted to give Hugh his best shot. Brother Hugh.

2

Jackie Kasey had met Brother Hugh on an airplane. Just like Wentworth said. Wentworth had told
Jackie Kasey that he would meet a very important
person on an airplane. A 747. The first-class compart-
ment. Jackie Kasey trusted Wentworth. Wentworth
was a mystic. She read Jackie's palm. She found his
fortune in the cards. She felt vibrations. She was a
comfort and Jackie Kasey was a seeker after comfort.
He went to a psychiatrist. His wife Roxy went to a
psychiatrist. He and his wife Roxy went to group
therapy. He and his wife Roxy and their four kids went
to family therapy. It did not leave many evenings free.
　　Wentworth's real name was not Wentworth.
Her real name was Hilda Suyker and she came from
Camden, New Jersey, and she was not a full-time practicing mystic. She lived with her mother and her mother
was eighty-six years old and her mother required a
certain amount of care. Wentworth was the kind of
mystic who went to Vegas on her vacations. It was a
change of pace from Camden, New Jersey. On one of
her trips she had wanted to meet Elvis but Elvis was not
receiving mystics during that engagement and so she
met Jackie Kasey. She read his palm and looked at the
cards and prophesied big things. In a very short while.
His shot, as in "see-your-shot-and-take-it." It was the
sort of thing Jackie Kasey liked to hear. He was making
three or four grand a week warming up for Elvis but in
Vegas three or four grand a week is welfare. He would
call Wentworth a couple of times a month at her home
in Camden, New Jersey, and they would talk about his
big shot and when it was coming. "Soon," Wentworth

would say, but she did not like to be pinned down as to when "soon" was. It was just soon.

In the spring Jackie went to play a date at the La Americana in Grover Hill, New Jersey. Grover Hill, New Jersey, was not far from Camden, New Jersey, and Jackie could spend a lot of time with Wentworth. Jackie was depressed. He was breaking in his Brother JayJay act at the La Americana and it did not seem all pulled together. It had possibilities, but it was not working, it did not seem like the big shot. Wentworth told Jackie not to worry. He would meet a man on an airplane. It was in the cards, in the bisecting lines on the palm. And the man he would meet on an airplane would help make him a household name. In all fifty states, the District of Columbia, Puerto Rico and American Samoa. The man would take charge of Jackie's career. Manage him. Package him. Package all that warmth and goodness and star quality.

Except for the hours with Wentworth, the eleven days at the La Americana in Grover Hill, New Jersey, were the worst in Jackie Kasey's life. The act was terrible, there was nowhere to go, nothing to do. The whole trip was a bummer. Wentworth would not tell him when he would meet the very important man on an airplane. Soon. That was all she said. Like with the big break. Next week, next month, next year. That was why Jackie Kasey did not notice the man at first. It just seemed too soon.

It was on the flight back to Los Angeles from Grover Hill, New Jersey. The man was wearing a gray flannel suit. And a white shirt. With a button-down collar. And a striped tie. And oxblood cordovans. And short hair. And no sideburns. A businessman. An executive. An important man, Jackie Kasey could tell.

The man's name was Hugh Hill and he was in the frosty-cream business. Not ice cream, not ice milk, frosty cream. Franchises. In fact Hugh Hill was new to the frosty-cream franchise business. Fortyish. How old are you, someone would ask Hugh Hill and he would reply, Fortyish. He had been a broker in New York, successful, five days a week from Darien to Wall Street and back, one wife, three children and no coronaries. Tennis was his game, doubles his specialty. Hugh Hill always tried to be a little better than his partner. Just enough better so that the partner knew that Hugh Hill was carrying him. There was nothing overt, nothing to get the partner irritated. It was just that Hugh Hill always liked to have an edge, even on his doubles partners.

The edge. It was how Hugh Hill got into the frosty-cream business. His brokerage house underwrote the frosty-cream company when it went public. Hugh Hill handled the refinancing and to safeguard the brokerage's investment he suggested himself as the frosty-cream company's chief executive officer. Always the edge. Hugh Hill did not know anything about the frosty-cream franchise business nor did he particularly care anything about it. But he was in his late thirties, he had not yet made a million dollars and the market was beginning to go soft. It was time to get out, and it was best to get out on top, even if it was on top of a frosty-cream company. Yogi Berra was the front man for a chocolate-drink company and Hugh Hill figured he was at least as smart as Yogi Berra. His contemporaries on the Street regarded the move as socially and professionally eccentric, like leaving the presidency of General Motors to manufacture enema tubes. But during the next eighteen months Hugh Hill's former brokerage house perished in the great bear market while Hugh Hill himself did very well indeed. He was working on his second million dollars, he had divorced his wife, moved to California and was living in a three-bedroom condominium in Playa del Rey. The condominium had a view of the Pacific Ocean and a round bed in the master bedroom on which a Bunny from the Playboy Club in Hollywood had once copped Hugh Hill's joint. There's this chick I know at the Playboy Club, Hugh Hill would say, and when he finished the story, he would shake his head and smile and add, It's a long way from Darien, Connecticut. Merchandising and promotion, that was what Hugh Hill was good at and he was reasonably sure that he would soon be edging in on his third million. The advertising agency he used also handled Bank of Savings and Peter Partridge Peanut Butter, solid commercial accounts plus what Hugh Hill called the fun-type things. The frosty-cream business was a fun-type thing.

Hugh Hill went to Vegas a lot to unwind. Pop over, see a couple of shows, take the late plane back, it was like a week's vacation. Don Rickles, Totie Fields, Robert Goulet, the superstars. Elvis' dinner show. It was at Elvis' dinner show that Hugh Hill saw Jackie Kasey for the first time. Jackie was Elvis' warm-up and Hugh Hill thought, N.G. "N.G." was a Hugh Hill expression. No good, no go. It cut through a lot of shit to say "N.G.," it headed off a lot of argument. If Hugh Hill did not like an ad campaign, he would tell the agency "N.G." just that, nothing more, and if they persisted, he would say, "I'm selling the frosty cream and I say it's 'N.G.' " Jackie Kasey was N.G. First there was the Polish routine. It was not that Hugh Hill minded Polish jokes. As a matter of fact he liked Polish jokes, he liked to ask, "Why does it take five Poles to change a light bulb?" and then to answer, "One to hold the bulb, four to turn the ladder." It was Polish dialect routines he did not like, there was something about a Jewish comic putting on a Polish accent that turned Hugh Hill off. It was all right for a K of C smoker, but not for Vegas. No class, N.G. And then there was Jackie Kasey's tuxedo. A brown Victorian number that came down to his knees. With a brown velours collar. Not velvet, velours. Hugh Hill had firm ideas about what a comic should wear onstage. A blazer. A suit. A certain kind of tuxedo: black watermark pattern, shawl collar, black piping. It spelled comic. A brown Victorian job with a bittersweet-chocolate velours collar, that was for the Oddfellows Hall, for the annual Paterson, N.J., High School football banquet. Not for Vegas. Hugh Hill wrote Jackie Kasey off. N.G.

They got talking the way people do on airplanes.
"Always fly United?" Hugh Hill said.
"TWA usually," Jackie Kasey said.
"TWA booked up?"
"Better movie on United."
"Ann-Margret," Hugh Hill said.
"Big jugs, if you know what I mean."
"I know what you mean."
"Ho, ho, he knows what I mean. He likes the big hogans."

•   •   •

By this time they were over Pittsburgh.

"It's better flying west," Jackie Kasey said.

"The time change makes it easier," Hugh Hill said.

"That's the truth."

"And the food's better flying west, for some reason."

"They got Trader Vic's on United now. Hawaiian food," Jackie Kasey said.

"Polynesian," Hugh Hill said.

"Hawaiian, too, though."

"I guess it's all the same."

"You like the Trader Vic tidbits?"

"Terrific. No spareribs, though."

"Try the crab puff."

"Good?"

"Tuh-riffic," Jackie Kasey said.

"You sound like Peter Falk you say 'Tuh-riffic.' "

By this time they were over Chicago.

"I'm not reading my *Time,* you want to look at it?" Hugh Hill said.

"I got *Variety,*" Jackie Kasey said.

"You in show business?"

By Council Bluffs, Iowa, they were on a first-name basis, by Denver they had a deal.

Hugh Hill said he had to be truthful. "The fact is, I didn't recognize you. The fact is, I didn't like the act in Vegas."

And Jackie Kasey had said, "The fact is, I'm

changing it. I got a whole new concept. That's what I was doing at the La Americana. It went terrific. They loved it, they want me back, name my own deal. A man's got to grow."

And Hugh Hill had said, "Gee, that's terrific. I'd like to see the new concept."

And Jackie Kasey had said, "Gee, I got a copy of it right here, Hugh, you want to read it?"

"That would be terrific, Jackie."

Hugh Hill saw the possibilities in the Brother JayJay concept immediately. He knew the concept needed work, it had to be rethought, but that was not the point, you could buy writers to do that, hire a director to stage the act. But the point was that the character of Brother JayJay was marketable, a commodity, like frosty cream. And if there was one thing Hugh Hill knew, it was merchandising. And if there was one thing he knew about merchandising, it was that it was easier to merchandise a character than a person. Jackie Kasey was nothing, but Brother JayJay, that was another matter. A television special first, then a television series, all built around Brother JayJay. A kind of raffish Howdy Doody. A comic prodigal son. The promotion possibilities were endless. Toys, dolls, T-shirts, sweatshirts, novelties, wrist watches, games, cards, photo blow-ups, greeting cards, pencil boxes, notebooks, lunch boxes. And those were just off the top of Hugh Hill's head.

Somewhere over Lincoln, Nebraska, the thought occurred to Hugh Hill that he might buy the concept from Jackie Kasey, buy it and fit it to another comic, someone more in the raffish mold, someone who did not tell Polish dialect stories, but he abandoned that idea quickly. Not out of any sense of scruple. It was just that the only comic he had ever met was sitting next to him in Seat 7-B in the first-class section of United's Flight 604 from Philadelphia to Los Angeles. And in the frosty-cream business one did not get a chance to meet many comics.

The truth of the matter was that Hugh Hill was just a little bored with the frosty-cream business. It was too easy, a million, nearly two, in eighteen months, that was fine, but a man needed other outlets, a way to express himself in creative-type things. It was a fact, though Hugh Hill would never admit it publicly, that people did not look up to someone in the frosty-cream business. People he liked, people he played tennis with, people who only made $32,500 a year, they would smile when he said he was in the frosty-cream business. Just a little smile, just a cracking at the corners of the mouth, but Hugh Hill did not like that little smile from people who bought their Hotpoint refrigerators on time. From people on revolving credit at the May Company. There was a television producer Hugh Hill played tennis with, a producer who had been out of work for eighteen months, ever since his last series was canceled after thirteen weeks, a producer whose name had been posted for nonpayment of his bar bills and who had borrowed $1,500 from Hugh Hill, and no one smiled at him when he talked about Vince Edwards and Dick and Penni Crenna and Danny and Rosalie Thomas and Bill Persky and Sam Denoff. He was in show business and someone in show business, even if he was tapped out, well, he somehow had more stature than someone in the frosty-cream business.

Hugh Hill asked the stewardess for a piece of paper, but all she had was a cocktail napkin, so he sketched out his proposition on the back of the napkin, the one with the United Airlines logo.

"How much money did you make last year, Jackie?"

"A hundred and eight grand."

"Okay, the first two fifty is yours, okay?"

"Okay."

"After two fifty, we split fifty-fifty."

"Okay."

"In other words, you make five hundred, then you keep the first two fifty, we split the next two fifty, you keep one twenty-five and I keep one twenty-five, that means your total is three seventy-five and mine is one twenty-five."

"You really think I can make five hundred a year, Hugh?"

"I wouldn't be in this if I didn't think that, Jackie."

Which was true. There was no point in branching out from the frosty-cream business unless there was money in it. And authority. Hugh Hill made that point crystal-clear. If he was going to package Brother JayJay, then he was in charge, he called all the shots. Booking, promotion, publicity, managing, investments, all the artistic decisions.

Jackie Kasey was delighted. "I used to have to do all that stuff myself," he said.

"All you got to worry about now is going on-stage," Hugh Hill said. "Showing up on time and going onstage. I'll take care of the rest."

"You can handle it?"

"Jackie, I've made two million dollars in the frosty-cream business. You don't make two million dollars unless you can cut the mustard. Promotion, merchandising, that's the ticket."

United 604 was landing in Los Angeles.

"You know, Wentworth told me I was going to meet someone like you," Jackie Kasey said. "On a plane, too."

"Who's Wentworth?"

Jackie Kasey got vague. It was too hard to explain. Someone with two million dollars might not understand a mystic in Camden, New Jersey.

"A friend of mine," Jackie Kasey said.

3

There were only forty-two people in for the second show the night before. Jackie Kasey knew the number exactly. He had started to count them out loud from the stage. He thought it would be a funny bit and then he got interested, twenty-eight, twenty-nine, thirty, the two ladies at the bar, that's thirty-two, good evening ladies, happy hunting, remember the wage-price freeze, thirty-three, thirty-four, the problem was none of the forty-two stiffs thought it was very funny. Fuck them. The sign wasn't big enough, that was it, if they had a big sign they could pull in two hundred people, even on a slow night. A comic's not like a singer, a singer can perform in front of nobody, in a goddam shower, for Chrissake, but a comic needs to tailor his art, he needs the warmth, the feedback. Maybe The Charioleers had

the right idea. The Charioleers were a comedy team
that filled in on swing nights when one of the headliners
had the night off, and the night before they had bought
their own electronic warmth. A laugh machine. Total
feedback. They told a joke and if the audience didn't
laugh, on went the laugh machine. Full volume.

"You hear about the Polish dog?"

"No, I didn't hear about the Polish dog."

"Broke his nose running after a parked car."

The laugh track echoed off the walls of the
empty lounge.

"Let's hear it for the laugh machine," one of
The Charioleers said.

The laugh machine giggled.

"I got bigger laughs than that on Death Row."

The laugh machine exploded.

"A fag kissed me the other night and you know
what he said?"

"No, what did the fag say?"

" 'Love means never having to say you're
sorry.' "

The laugh machine roared.

The trick was not to panic. No matter it was like
playing the city morgue: don't panic. There were two
drunks down front. Play to them. That was the trick.
Always play to somebody. So what if they don't laugh.
The act works, that's what's important. You're terrific,
Jackie, one drunk said. Terrific, the other drunk said.
Brother Hugh should have seen that, the way he played
to those drunks. Drunks were one thing, however, the
blonde was another. Jee-zuss, the blonde. She was sitting by herself, a blonde with a lot of mileage, she
looked ready for her 18,000-mile check, lube and minor

tune. A live one, someone to play off. The mistake was sitting down at her table.

"Watching the ice melt?"

The blonde did not acknowledge him.

"Got a date with your swizzle stick?"

The blonde did not move.

"You want to be saved?"

The blonde spoke. "Buzz off."

"Now, sister . . ."

"Beat it." Loud. Very loud. No laugh machine to drown it out. "You read me?" Louder still. "Beat it."

Clap those hands. Save the situation. Play to the Lord. The Man Upstairs is always good for a chuckle.

"The Lord says the secret of salvation is to let people be what they wants to be. The Lord said that, yes, he did. To my grandfather. Rufus T. Beauregard. Brother Rufus. On a train. Between Waxahachie, Texas, and Tallahassee, Florida. A freight. The Lord was traveling economy class. With Brother Rufus. And this railroad detective, he opens up the door of the freight car, and the Lord says to my granddaddy, 'Rufus, what do you want to be?' And Brother Rufus says, 'Out of here.' "

Raise the finger. "That is what the Good Book calls a parable. And that parable applies to this sister here. Now, this sister wants to be alone and the Lord will grant her wish."

Eyes toward heaven. Get the purple spot up there, for Christ's sake.

"Won't you, Lord?"

A chorus of "The Battle Hymn of the Republic" and then an Italian joke. It wasn't Brother JayJay but he couldn't think of anything else to say, so he told it in a Brother JayJay accent.

"The Lord say to me, 'Jay, you know the three times in his life when an Italian sees his priest?'

"And I say to Him, 'Tell me, Lord.'

"And He say to me, 'When he's baptized, when he's married and when they strap him into the electric chair.'

"And I say to Him, 'Amen, Lord.' "

Upstairs in his dressing room he turned on the vaporizer for his cold and sucked on a bottle of Mountain Valley mineral water. Elvis drank Mountain Valley. It was good for the colon, Colonel Parker said. It would beat the shit out of colitis. So the blonde didn't laugh. The act was working, he knew it like he knew he had a hole in his tush. He put on a mauve jump suit. The zipper had a gold ring on it, like a ripcord of a parachute. Get the car washed, take some steam, get the throat sprayed. That would take care of Tuesday.

There must have been three million people in the casino. And only forty-two could make it into his second show. If only there was a big name playing the main room. You get a superstar in the main room, a real heavyweight, it's got to help the lounge, they come out of the show, they're feeling good, they stop by your room to unwind. Not that Cosby wasn't a superstar. But he was a *schwartze* and nobody wanted to listen to that black bullshit anymore. That's what Si Miller said. Si Miller ran junkets in from Pittsburgh and the junkets from Pittsburgh were a class operation, every guy a high roller good for at least six, seven grand for the junket, not bad for three days in Vegas, and these guys were up to here with the *schwartze* shit.

"Always the *schtup* on race," Si Miller had said.

"The beard and all that bullshit," Jackie Kasey had said.

"The Panthers."

"People don't want to hear that shit."

"Not your Pittsburgh people."

"He'll learn."

"He's got to."

Red Salomon was in with the Pittsburgh junket. There was a Red Salomon in every town. A guy who loved comics. A guy who loved to hang around show people. They send you up a card, they buy you a drink, they have you by the house for dinner. Pretty soon they're your best friend in Pittsburgh, Pa., or Canton, Ohio. The Red Salomon of Canton, Ohio, was a guy named Mike Cusick. Mike was the son of the biggest undertaker in Canton and Mike said that when you worked with stiffs all day you liked to have a few laughs at night. That was why Mike Cusick liked comics. Some of the comics who worked Canton, he liked to say, reminded him of the stiffs he pumped full of formaldehyde all day. Formaldehyde jobs, he called them. The Club Victor in Canton, Ohio, Jackie Kasey thought. The first time he played the Victor Mike Cusick took him under his wing. Mike Cusick was some kind of hunky and he said that Jackie Kasey was the real thing, he said the Dangerous Dan, the Used Car Man routine just broke him up. Mike Cusick had seen a lot of formaldehyde jobs at the Club Victor, but Jackie was total talent, Jackie was going to go through the roof. He would sit down front, this big hunky with the funny smell from handling formaldehyde all day, and if anyone tried to heckle him, Mike Cusick would stand

up and say, "Let Jackie do his act." It always did the
trick, there weren't that many people in Canton who
wanted to tangle with some big hunky who smelled of
formaldehyde. There wasn't anything Mike Cusick
wouldn't do for a comic he liked. You needed a writer?
Mike Cusick would buy you a writer, bring him out
from New York, all expenses paid while he was in
Canton, fifteen hundred bucks it cost him. There were-
n't many writers in New York ready for a gig in Canton, Ohio, but Mike Cusick put an ad in *Variety* and
this writer answered, he had staged shows in Atlanta
and Miami Beach, and Mike Cusick brought him out
to the Club Victor, Christmas 1962. A washer, a dryer,
a refrigerator, furniture—Mike Cusick always knew
someone in the wholesale business who owed him a
favor, maybe because he planted the guy's mother-in-
law for a cut rate. Mike Cusick would not accept payment. Just knowing a guy like you, that's all the payment I need, Mike Cusick would say. Or he would say,
How about a little golf on Saturday, my insurance man,
he's never met a superstar. It made Jackie a little uncomfortable to think of Mike Cusick. It must be seven
years since he talked to him. Not since he stopped
playing the Club Victor. You grow, Jackie Kasey
thought, and I guess you forget.
    "Jackie Kasey."
    Jackie Kasey thought, Who the fuck is this.
Give it time, the thinker never fails, squat, bald, red
face, smoking a cigar, carrying a drink, red cardigan,
clap the hands, snap the fingers, aim it like a gun, here
it comes: "Red Salomon."
    "Jackie."
    "Red."

"Haven't changed a bit."

"Neither have you."

"Jackie."

What to say next. Make it good. There's a Red Salomon in every town. "What're you doing in Vegas, Red?"

"On a junket, Jackie. Wait'll I tell the boys. There's a bunch here from Pittsburgh."

"Remember the Arcadia Gardens?"

"Remember the Arcadia Gardens? Does a bear shit in the woods?"

"Last time I heard."

"Jackie."

"Red."

"Listen, Jackie, I saw Vic at the Holiday House . . ."

"Vic?"

"Damone."

"No shit, how's Vic?"

"He's broken through, Jackie. You know, there was always something missing. Not the pipes. He always had the pipes, but there was always something holding him back. Well, I want to tell you something, Jackie, not now. Vic has clicked. When I saw him at the Holiday House he was a real superstar. No looking back, none of that 'On the Street Where You Live' shit. A new act, a new personality. The only thing he hasn't changed are the pipes and Frank always said he had the best pipes in the business."

"Frank said that?"

"The chairman of the board himself, Francis Albert Sinatra."

"No shit?"

"No shit."

"Gee, Red, I'm glad."

"Jackie."

"Red."

"I'll call you."

"Room 2556."

Jackie Kasey thought, Red Salomon. Red and Vic, Red and Frank. Excuse me, Red and the Chairman of the Board. Red Salomon. When Liberace played the Holiday House, Red Salomon was calling him Lee before the second show opening night. Steve and Edie, Shecky, Buddy, Jackie, Joey, everyone who played Pittsburgh knew Red Salomon. There's a Red Salomon in every town. You want to play some handball, Red Salomon will play some handball with you, you want to take some steam, Red Salomon will take some steam with you. Want a girl, Red Salomon knows a manicurist, a terrific kid, a great fuck and she'll stay out of your hair. Jackie Kasey wondered what Red Salomon did. Besides buying drinks at the Arcadia Gardens and the Holiday House, that is. It's funny I never asked, Jackie Kasey thought. He must be doing good though, Red.

FOURTEEN

I met her at a party off the pier in Venice. I had gone home for the weekend and right away I wished I had stayed in Vegas. First there was the construction. We were adding a room onto the house and what had started as a two-month job was now stretching into its sixth month and the construction account was four thousand dollars overdrawn. The first night home I fired the contractor. "Jesus, man, I understand," he said. He was an out-of-work actor and his crew sniffed a lot of cocaine and when he left he unexpectedly gave me a soul brother handshake, grabbing my thumb while I was left with an unimportant part of his little finger. That night my wife and I agreed to sell the house and to get a divorce. In the morning it occurred to me that the house was unsellable. There was a half-finished bedroom and partially laid tile on the living-room floor, and until the new French doors were put in, only a sheet of clear pliofilm separated us from the Pacific Ocean. The pliofilm blew in the wind. I rehired the contractor. "Jesus, man, I understand," the contractor said. One of his crew lit a joint and began

to scar the concrete block on which the tile was being
laid with a jackhammer. The noise from the jackhammer made my daughter cry and my wife said she would
take her to Sacramento that morning and I said I would
go back to Vegas the next day. That night I went to the
party in Venice.

It was a terrible party at the apartment of someone I did not know. Cinder-block bookcases full of
Hesse and Tolkien. Gallon jugs of Almadén Mountain
Red, plastic cups and no ice. It was like all those terrible
parties in the Village in the fifties. A girl in a batik skirt
was rolling joints and someone said, The Army taught
me the positive value of hate, and someone else said, I
resented it when they made me a PFC, and an older
black woman in an oatmeal-colored sheath said, I grew
up in the swirl and dash of the Sartre-Camus debates,
nothing like that today, nothing, *nada.*

Finito.

Kaput.

Finished.

Big Sur, San Miguel, Manitoba, Maui. Everyone
there was about to "split," everyone there was "into"
something. The girl I had just met was into cryogenics.

"I heard they're keeping Walt Disney on ice,"
she said.

Someone said she was Leibowitz's chick and she
said her name was Deborah Doty and she said she was
thirty-four years old and she said she was sick of this
shit and she asked if I would take her home.

We had some sand dabs at the Soft Shell on
Washington Street in Venice and then I drove her up
the coast to her house in Topanga Canyon. There was
a man in the living room in tie-dyed jeans cleaning a
kilo of marijuana.

"This is Ron," Deborah Doty said.

Ron said, "Hi," and grabbed my thumb, but this time I was ready for it. Ron picked up the grass and the strainer and the bowl and gave me the peace symbol and disappeared into the bedroom.

"Who's Ron?"

"Ron's cool."

"Who's Leibowitz?"

"A schmuck."

She said she was a ghost writer. That was how she got into cryogenics. She was ghosting a book for a man who had made a world-wide study of cryogenics and this man knew about a number of very famous and very important stiffs who were on ice, a lot more important than Walt Disney.

Ron came back into the living room and said he wanted to lay a joint on us. He took a hit himself and then went back into the bedroom.

"He's my ex-husband," Deborah Doty said.

"Oh."

"He's into sound. You know, for movies."

I nodded.

"We share expenses. It's cheap. We've got season tickets to the Rams' games. We've only made it once in seven years. After the Rams-Cardinals game. We dropped acid at half time. We go our own way type thing."

"I like that type thing."

She was from Minneapolis and she had run away from home when she was fifteen. She made her way to a resort in Brainerd, Minnesota, where she got a job as a waitress. She was a virgin, but as her parents had already set private detectives on her trail, she decided that she should just as well be hung for a sheep as a goat. So she balled the first guy who asked her. He was the social director at the resort.

"A comic, too," she said. "He emceed the Saturday night show. Awful."

"What was his name?"

"You never heard of him."

But already I knew I had.

"Jackie Kasey," she said.

2

"No shit," Jackie Kasey said.

"It happened," I said. "It really happened."

"Debby Doty." He seemed pleased. "And she remembered me?"

"Absolutely."

"I guess you never forget your first fuck."

"I guess not."

"Debby Doty." He opened a bottle of Mountain Valley mineral water. "To tell the truth I don't remember her."

We were sitting in his suite on the twenty-fifth floor of the hotel. The bedroom was a riot of red-flocked wallpaper, like something viewed in a pathologist's microscope. There was a king-sized canopy bed and under the lace and fringe canopy there was a full-length antiqued mirror. I tried to imagine how management allotted the rooms with the mirrors under the canopies. Did they have a master list of high rollers who liked to do it with mirrors? Was there a poll that said mirror men were good players?

The suite's living room was across a closed-off

corridor. Jackie Kasey rarely used it. In fact the suite was only a suite at all when the hotel was not crowded. On weekends or when there was a big convention in town, the hotel let out the living room, leaving Jackie with only the smaller of the two rooms. Ten thousand dollars a week and he still had to give up his living room on weekends to some dentist from East Holt Avenue in Pomona with a wife who looked as if she washed her hair in Sani-Flush. It seemed the ultimate mark of the semi-name. He tried to rationalize. You see, they've got this ninety-seven percent occupancy rate here, and volume, that's the name of the game in Vegas today.

I thought of someone trying to lay the ninety-seven percent occupancy rate on Elvis.

Miss Nevada had got the day off to a bad start. Hey, come on over, Jackie Kasey had said when he called early that morning. Watch me be photographed with Miss Nevada. It was, he said, a personal favor for the chief of police. To give the kid a head start in the Miss America contest. Or the Miss Universe contest. Jackie Kasey was not sure which. I had never met a beauty queen and I immediately fantasized sexual adventure. A hot shower, a splash of bay rum. Miss Nevada. The very words conjured up a nest of pubic hair. I would use my connections with Jackie Kasey to bang Miss Nevada. As part of the story, of course. And then Jackie Kasey would have something on me. It was a soothing thought.

Only there was no Miss Nevada. Just a fat photographer lying on the floor of the living room pointing his Nikon at the navel of a vapid teenager. She was perhaps seventeen, with bangs and a Dust Bowl face, and she was wearing a black mini and high white vinyl

boots and over her white nylon tricot blouse was a piece
of cheap pink ribbon on which was printed, in gold
letters, JR. MISS F.O.P.A., LODGE NO. 1.

I asked her what the F.O.P.A. was. She
shrugged and shook her head. Her eyes never seemed
to blink and her jaws worked methodically over a wad
of gum.

From the floor the photographer said that the
F.O.P.A. was the Fraternal Order of Police Associa-
tions and that Lodge No. 1 was sponsoring an off-road
motorcycle race a month hence for the Policemen's
Death Benefit Fund.

"Out of sight," the girl said.

"They told me she was Miss Nevada," Jackie
Kasey said.

"Maybe she's in training for Miss Nevada," the
photographer said. "Look at Jackie, sweetheart."

"Yeah, maybe she's in training for Miss
Nevada," Jackie Kasey said. "You in training for Miss
Nevada, sweetheart?"

Jr. Miss F.O.P.A. shook her head. "Uh-uh," she
said.

Instant soft-on, Jackie Kasey called the girl
later. That she was not Miss Nevada seemed to nettle
him. And so I had told him about Debby Doty. Anything to raise his spirits, even an unremembered liaison
of twenty years before. He had all but forgotten the
resort in Brainerd, Minnesota. A-Tos-Ennim Lodge,
that was it. Not a real Indian name, just Minnesota
spelled backward. There were not that many Jews in
Minnesota but the single ones all seemed to show up at
A-Tos-Ennim in the summer. Secretaries from St. Paul,
bank tellers from Minneapolis, IBM operators from

Duluth. You signed your contract and the entertainment director shook your hand and gave you a big wink, and the big wink meant, You do one show a night and boff everyone you can lay a hand on. Keep the broads happy. That was part of the lure of A-Tos-Ennim for the dental technician from Rochester. Romance in the Land of the 10,000 Lakes. One-twenty a week, American Plan; a two-week fling courtesy of the Vacation Club. That was what was funny about Debby Doty, she being a waitress and all. You weren't supposed to boff the hired help, just the paying customers. That was what they were there for, a roll in the pine needles under the Minnesota moon. Hey, what's your name? Edna, Edna what? Edna Slotkin? That's a cute name, Edna Slotkin. I like Irish names, what you doing tonight, Edna? Life was simple at the A-Tos-Ennim Lodge. There were no telegrams from Hugh Hill, no one asking you to be photographed with Miss Nevada as a personal favor to the chief of police.

3

"It's a special color," Melinda said. "Pearl-white. They don't make pearl-white Porsches any more. But there's this place in Barstow, they'll give you a pearl-white paint job. It's so beautiful, just like acrylic. I've always wanted a white car. You can see it on the desert at night. It's like it floats on the sand. That's the beauty of a Porsche. It can do ninety in second gear."

She was nineteen and she was stroking the inside of Jackie Kasey's thigh. She lived with her mother on the golf course at the Desert Inn Country Club and her

father had points on the Strip and it was best not to ask
how he got the points or why he was now in Colombia
running a casino on the coast for the People. She was
blond and pretty, long straight hair, not teased, a soap
and water girl, and she had met Jackie Kasey in Los
Angeles. She knew a lot of people in L.A., it was her
kind of town, four hours and five minutes from the
Desert Inn to L.A. in the Porsche. She liked the Dunge-
ness crab at Jack's at the Beach and the bullshots at the
Polo Lounge and she liked to go to the Academy
Awards at Santa Monica Civic, past the grandstands
full of fans, that was what L.A. was all about. But best
of all she liked her Porsche, she liked the tachometer
and the stick shift, she liked to floor it in the desert, 130
flat-out. Once she had raced a CHP cruiser from Baker
to the Nevada line, his siren was pumping, his red light
blinking, it was beautiful, like a ballet, and when she
crossed into Nevada, she stopped her Porsche, the old
cordovan-red Porsche, and walked back to the state line
and rapped with the CHP officer. He was good about
losing the race to the state line, he did not mind at all,
those old Ford Galaxies did not have that much juice,
but he said she should watch out for the Nevada Highway Patrol, those old boys were not as tolerant as the
CHP. His name was Bob and he lived in Barstow and
she promised to call him up the next time she passed
through Barstow.

    "I ought to do that," Melinda said. "I really
ought." Her voice was dreamlike and her hand still
stroked the inside of Jackie Kasey's thigh. "I never
made it with a cop." She smiled. "As a matter of fact
I never made it in Barstow."

    She began to sing "Eleanor Rigby" and disap-
peared into the bathroom.

"I never made it with her," Jackie Kasey said. "Honest."

Jackie was already sick of her and he was sick of me, which is why he had called her in the first place. Melinda was going to inherit points on the Strip, Melinda was class, even if her thinker was set on making it with a highway patrolman in Barstow, but she could get into Jack's at the Beach without a reservation and she knew Maury Green at the Beverly Hills Hotel and Maury would always fix her up with a little suite, no matter it was Oscar weekend and the nominees were all flying in from location in Mindoro or Kabul with their agents and their press agents and their personal managers and their business managers, all those guys who took the first fifty-five percent of your income to keep you from going bankrupt, all those guys and their girl friends and their boy friends, it was always surprising to Jackie how many personal managers were fags (you know the difference between a queer and a fag, he would say, my son's queer, your son's a fag, it always got a laugh in the lounge), crowded did not matter to Maury Green when Melinda was in town, her daddy had points on the Strip, major points, and Melinda was class and class was what Jackie Kasey did not find an awful lot of in Vegas that day. He wondered if the sandwich chef stopped Cosby in the casino and gave him jokes too, jokes about *whoors,* that was the way the sandwich chef pronounced it, *whoors,* or jokes about *poop,* that was what he called shit, *poop,* making it sound cute while he passed out the free hotdogs and the tiny chunks of roast beef at the cocktail-hour sandwich bar in the casino.

"Gee, that's great, Freddy," he would say to the sandwich chef. "I'll put it in my card file under 'poop,'

I got this three-by-five index-card file of poop jokes."

He was always a special favorite of the sandwich chefs and the bartenders, all the people whom he reverently called the little people on the talk shows, as in, "You can't survive in this town without the little people, if you don't have them in your corner you can forget it," little people who would understand what it was like to give up half your suite on big weekends to a *macher* from Pomona, but the price was he had to listen to their poop jokes and to their schemes.

"You got thirty days open, Jackie?" The speaker was Sammy, the bartender at the hotel's Punahou Café, a specialist in grasshoppers and gin slings and frozen daiquiris; anything made with a Waring blender Sammy could whip up better than anyone on the Strip.

"I don't understand you, Sammy," Jackie Kasey said. His face was set as if he was preparing to catch another poop joke.

"The thing is, would you like to play Honolulu?" Sammy said.

"Hey, yeah, Sammy, I'd like to play Honolulu."

"At Don Ho's?"

"Sure, at Don Ho's. He's a big talent, Don."

"Well, here's the thing," Sammy said. He topped a pair of grasshoppers and set them on a tray. "My brother-in-law was best man at Don's sister's wedding. She married Gene Lerner. You know Gene, Jackie?"

Jackie Kasey shook his head.

"He's got the Jack-in-the-Box franchises in the Western Pacific," Sammy said. He wore rimless glasses and his face sagged with defeat. "Wake, Guam, you know. Okinawa. So I'm a very dear personal friend of Don's."

"Gee, I didn't know that, Sammy."

"So I could get in touch with Don for you, Jackie."

Jackie Kasey's face was closing like an automatic door. "Yeah, sure, Sammy."

"I could get ahold of Gene and Gene's wife could call Don."

"That's great."

"Maybe you could get in touch with Don. Tell him you met me. How my brother-in-law was best man at his sister's wedding."

"How do I get in touch?"

"He's got these two addresses. I'll give you the private address. You stamp the letter 'personal' and I'll guarantee you it'll get to him. You don't stamp 'personal,' you're in trouble, you see, he's got this really nosy secretary and she tears up stuff she doesn't want him to see, even Christmas cards."

"I'll write him, Sammy."

He looked around warily, as if he expected a bellhop to hit him with an oil-well deal, and shrugged, as if to say, What are you going to do. The first thing he did was turn around and touch the hair of the girl sitting at the next table. "Nice hair, what color is it?" Jackie Kasey said.

"Dark brown, I guess," the girl said. She looked as if strange men had been touching her hair in bars since puberty. "There's some who call it auburn."

"Where you from?"

"Here."

"Where do you work?"

"No place."

"How do you make a living?"

"You know."

"I know." He let go her hair and turned back to his drink. "No class. Ten words and I can tell. I just got to hear her talk. No class."

No class. That was why he had called Melinda and now she was in the can humming "Eleanor Rigby" and he was sick of her and he was sick of me and he was sick of bartenders and sandwich chefs and girls with hair that some called auburn and he was especially sick of Hugh Hill and the fact that he was expected for dinner Thursday night. He turned on the television set, always moving, like a beagle in heat. There was a local talk show he had taped earlier that week and he wanted to watch it. The Jerry Fisher Show. Basically he told Jerry Fisher the same thing he had told Ramsey Tait, only he was wearing a different color jump suit and there was no fag singer from a tit show to share the air time with. Melinda came out of the can, into "Scarborough Fair" now, and she looked fresh and blond, like a Tri Delt at UNLV, and she said to me, "I love Jackie, but I never made it with him. I don't make it with entertainers."

Jackie Kasey said, "Shhh." He hunched in front of the television set, mouthing his dialogue. The patter was down so pat it was as if he were working from a script, with only the names of the talk-show hosts interchangeable. His image flickered on the screen. The image told Jerry Fisher about his wife Roxy. "She's the only person who's ever been honest with me, Jerry," the image said. "You and Roxy, you're the only two people, Jerry." A nice recovery. That should make Jerry feel good. "Roxy says, 'Jackie, I'm the only one who's ever honest with you.' And I say to her, 'Roxy, you and Jerry.' And so the night I opened Brother JayJay, I said

to her, 'Roxy, you're the only one I can really believe.'
And she said to me, 'Jackie, it worked.' "

Melinda ran her hand over the inside of my
thigh. "What did she really say?" Melinda said. At
nineteen she had already stored up a lifetime of Vegas
wisdom.

"She said it was shit," Jackie Kasey said.

FIFTEEN

Later, Melinda said, "Let's go to Barstow."

"It's three o'clock in the morning," I said.

"The night is young," Melinda said. She trailed a chiffon scarf across her face and smiled.

"It's two hundred fifty miles to Barstow," I said.

"One hundred fifty," Melinda said.

"What's in Barstow?" I said.

The chiffon scarf again. "I never made it in Barstow," Melinda said.

"So you said."

In fact I never went to Barstow with Melinda. Not out of any moral scruple. A jump in a Ramada Inn in Barstow, a ride back across the desert in a Porsche: there was no trouble-quotient. I was only interested in relationships with a trouble-quotient; my interest in them was exactly commensurate with my inability to handle them. Barstow with Melinda I could handle. Which is what made it out of the question.

I went home and called my wife. The phone rang nine times before she picked it up. Her voice was thick with sleep. "What time is it?" she said.

"After three."

"When are you coming home?"

"I don't know."

"And that's what you called to tell me. At three o'clock in the morning. When I was asleep."

"Tell me about your alpha waves."

Silence.

"And give me the routine about the positive ions." She had a theory that positive ions were the cause of all physical malaise. Negative ions were the "good" ions; one could partake of negative ions in a hot shower.

Silence.

"And a little on the Santa Ana."

Silence.

"And top it off with the number on premenstrual tension."

Silence.

"You got an ice bag?" She always slept with a plastic baggie filled with ice on top of her head. To ward off bad alpha waves, positive ions, PMT, the Santa Ana and all forms of bad karma. The ice bag usually leaked.

"I said, do you have an ice bag?"

She hung up. She had too high a trouble-quotient. Which was why, for the moment, she was out of the question.

I rolled a piece of paper into my typewriter. It was an old form of therapy. When depressed I would write suicide notes. I prided myself on their power, persuasiveness and malignant beauty. "I don't want you to go through the rest of your life," I would write, "with my death on your conscience." Or: "What happened is my fault, and only my fault." I never knew why

I was supposed to be committing suicide, or what event was supposed to be the last straw. It gave a mystical quality to the notes, some of which were of epic length. I would labor over them, correcting, revising, sharpening. Whatever minimal impulse I had for suicide was negated by the craft of writing the suicide note. It became a technical problem. I was manipulative, shouldering the bulk of the blame, pointing to the intolerable emotional duress I was under, but always there was the implication that she—it was always a she—was in some way responsible for the gas jet even then being on, that only my good breeding prevented me from casting any blame even while my breath grew short. Tears would come to my eyes. It was time to stop; the note was a success. Crumple it, throw it away; there is nothing more embarrassing the next morning than reading one of your own suicide notes. Especially for a suicide never contemplated.

I felt better. I went to sleep.

2

The second time Artha got busted she got hold of me and not her bail bondsman. It's nothing to get your rocks off about, she said. She only got one telephone call after being booked and when Bill Parsons' line was busy she called me. One dime, one call and hurry up about it. That was the way things operated in the tank downtown and if Bill Parsons was gabbing, then that was tough shit, lady, you better make another call quick or you're back in the cooz corner without any bail. So she called me and told me to get in touch with

Bill Parsons and have him haul ass downtown so that she could hit the bricks no later than eight the next morning. That was what really pissed her off, having to spend the night in the tank. It was only eleven thirty when she got pinched, but by the time she got downtown and they pulled her rap sheet it was after midnight and too late to get sprung. That meant a night in the tank watching a couple of dykes fingering each other and asking the other chicks if they wanted to join in. One of them was this big diesel and she whipped her finger out of the other chick's cooz and offered to let anyone in the mood cop a whiff. Fun stuff like that. The other thing that pissed her off was that the cop who made the pinch was the same vice who had busted her at the Landmark the first time. The tall dude in the Thom McAn shoes and the Ed's for Style suit and the middle linebacker haircut. Same shoes, same suit, different hotel.

The only reason she was even out was she had been having a little romance. With an honest-to-God fucking cowboy. From Big Springs, Texas. His name was Dale John. Not Dale, not John, Dale John. Dale John Lee, Jr. Dale John was a bronc rider in the rodeo playing the Convention Center. He had a girl friend named LuAnne Simms who was a barrel racer in the rodeo and a wife named Helen Mary who lived in Big Springs with their three boys. In a big Fleetwood mobile home. Dale John loved that Fleetwood mobile home a lot more than he did Helen Mary, but it was in her name and there was no way he could get her to change it over. Three bedrooms, two baths, plus den, wet bar and decorative fireplace. You could put logs in the fireplace and flick a switch and it was so real it looked like it was really burning. The Fleetwood was the reason for Dale John's fuss with LuAnne Simms. She wanted to move right into that Fleetwood back in Big Springs when the rodeo season was over. What she really meant was she wanted Dale John to kick Helen Mary's ass right on out of it, and this Dale John was not about to do as long as the Fleetwood was in Helen Mary's name. So LuAnne and Dale John had an argument in the chutes of the Convention Center and it ended up with LuAnne getting her nose broken. That was how Artha ended up with Dale John. One of the girls at the Manhattan Beauty College was banging the rodeo clown and the clown said that Dale John was at loose ends since LuAnne got her nose broken and the girl said she had a friend in tints named Artha. Dale John took to Artha right away. The first night he took a sixth in bronc riding and he was feeling bad about it, but Artha brought him home and fixed him some Polish sausage and he felt a lot better. He told Artha he had never had Polish sausage before and she told him she had never met a cowboy before and pretty soon they were fucking on the kitchen floor. The nice thing was that Dale John never knew that she was a hooker. The rodeo only had three days left in Vegas before it moved on to Prescott, Arizona, and so Dale John never gave much thought about what she did besides go to the Manhattan Beauty College. He said he was sure that there were a number of openings in the cosmetology field in the Big Springs area and he hoped that she would consider settling there. It was a pleasant place to live and a cosmetician would have no trouble financing a Fleetwood, one of the smaller models. Dale John liked the fact that she was going to be in the beauty-parlor

game. Helen Mary was slinging hamburgers at a Bob's
Big Boy in Wichita Falls when he first met her and
LuAnne Simms was a telephone operator out of Visalia,
California, before she became a barrel racer. There was
nothing, Dale John said, like having your own place of
business. Like being your own boss. Which you sure as
hell couldn't be, working for the telephone company or
Bob's Big Boy.

The day the rodeo left town Artha promised
Dale John that she would give every consideration to
the Big Springs area when it came time to pick a locale.
She gave him a Polish sausage and he gave her a pillow
on which was stitched "Calgary Stampede, 1969."
They promised to keep in touch. A couple of hours later
she was copping the joint of a guy at the Sands in on
a New Orleans junket. It seemed like everything was
going to work out terrific. She thought she was going
to have to cruise to make up for the three nights she was
with Dale John, but then she got a call from a guy she
knew whose father brought in junkets from St. Louis
and New Orleans. There was a junket in from New
Orleans and there were two guys in it from Jefferson
Parish who were dying to get laid after Joey Bishop's
dinner show. They were real fans of Joey's and they
liked to fuck before they went to the tables, they considered it good luck. Some guys only liked to do it after
playing, but these guys said what happens if you lose,
you can't get it up, so if you do it before and you lose,
at least you dropped a load. She had not seen Joey's
show and that meant dinner and a few laughs before
going upstairs and if she took on both guys from Jefferson Parish that was two hundred. Plus a steak.

The first thing she had to do was ball the guy

whose dad brought in the junkets. That was part of the package. A free piece of ass for his remembering to call. He banged her and then they watched *Outpost in Malaya* on the tube with Jack Hawkins and Claudette Colbert and then she got ready for the dinner show. It was nice not to have to cruise. She put on her best black velours pant suit and drove to the Sands in her Dodge Dart. The steak was good and Joey was never in better form. He had some good lines about Don Rickles and Johnny Carson and Rickles was in the audience and came up onstage and called Joey the meathead from Philadelphia. It was really funny and the two guys from Jefferson Parish said Joey was the funniest comic in Vegas and both of them put a hand on her pussy between courses. When the show broke they went right upstairs because both guys said they were anxious to get to the tables, they were really feeling lucky, and she gave each of them a little French and then they took turns fucking her, a minute for this guy, a minute for that one, then two, then three until both of them popped. It seemed like a contest, which one could hold it the longest. She was sure they had a bet on it, the way some guys bet on their golf scores, the guy who popped first had to buy dinner the next night or something like that. Anyway they were nice enough johns, both with a lot of hair on their backs, and they said they would call her again, and if she ever moved to New Orleans she could make a fortune, there just weren't girls like her in the Quarter. Which really made her laugh. Because that was the same thing Dale John had said about Big Springs, only he was talking about cosmetology.

It was early and she should have gone home, but she was short as a result of not working for three nights, even with the two hundred from the johns from Jefferson Parish, so she decided to make a short cruise of the casino looking for a quick trick. Nothing. A lot of lookers and one old guy who asked her the time, making a big deal out of it, you sure your watch is right, it's such a pretty little watch, and such a pretty little wrist it's on, he was just trying to think himself into a hard-on without paying for it. And then a guy at a blackjack table turned around and put a shoulder into her tit, giving her the big smile, EX-CUSE me, with all the teeth, as if he didn't know she had her boobs hanging all over his soft seventeen, as if he wasn't just trying to grab a shoulder feel. Fuck it, time to go home. Then right by the front door, there he was, the tall dude with the Thom McAn shoes and the Ed's For Style suit. Hi, he said, it's Artha, isn't it? Like he was going to get a merit badge or a person-to-person telephone call from President Nixon for remembering her name. You were very well coached, deputy. Thank you, Mr. President, we had a good game plan. There's an element we don't want in the Sands, deputy. That's right, Mr. President, nobody who might embarrass Mr. Bebe Rebozo. Ha ha, deputy. Thank you, Mr. President.

    I found Bill Parsons' name in the Yellow Pages under "Bonds—Bail." His quarter-page advertisement had two slogans, "I'll Get You Out of Jail and Onto the Street" and "Specialist in Bondage." I assumed he did not want anyone to miss the point. He said he would get Artha out the next morning, she was a good kid, it was a shame she had to spend the night in the cooler, that tank was a zoo unless you happened to be a diesel butch and maybe if I was downtown in the morning the

three of us could have a short stack together at the
Union Plaza, they had the best boysenberry syrup in
Vegas and the dollar-size wheatcakes were a treat.

Artha thought the boysenberry syrup was shit
and she didn't think much of the short stack either. A
night in the cooler and she's loaded for bear, they're all
like that, Bill Parsons said. She had a lot of juice in the
Tropicana pits, Artha said, and she was going to bust
that dude with the Dick Butkus haircut right back to
pushing traffic in Henderson. He's got clocks on his
socks, she said. He lives in a fucking trailer court, she
said. You sound like you got very tight with him, Bill
Parsons said. You should have given him a little head,
he might have dropped the charge, Bill Parsons said.
I'll give you a check for the fifty, Artha said. Forget it,
Bill Parsons said, this one's on me. He took a Union
Plaza room key from his pocket and gave it to her. Why
don't you go upstairs and get cleaned up, he said. Take
a shower. Grab a little nap. Room Service and all the
trimmings. I'll call you a little later.

Bill Parsons said he was a twenty-year man in
the Air Force, the last six at Nellis. He liked the climate
at Nellis and decided to settle in Vegas when he got out,
it seemed the right place for someone with his interests.
What he was interested in was singing, a show-business
career. The thing he wanted most when he was in the
Air Force was to be a member of the Singing Sergeants.
The Singing Sergeants sang at recruiting drives and the
Sugar Bowl game and at the Freedom Foundation in
Valley Forge, Pennsylvania, and at all kinds of patriotic
events. It was good duty with a lot of travel and the
chance to meet people in other fields than the Air
Force, successful people who weren't ashamed to cry

when they heard, "Off we go, Into the wild, blue yonder, Climbing high into the sky . . ." That was how the Singing Sergeants ended every concert, it was their theme song, the way "Over the Rainbow" was Judy Garland's theme song. Bill Parsons said he would have made the Singing Sergeants if there had not been a crisis in Berlin in the summer of 1961. He was scheduled for a tryout, but then his unit got orders to ship out and he lost his voice yelling at recruits new to crises with the Communists. The orders were finally canceled at the last moment, but by that time Bill Parsons' throat was so bad he had to pull out of his audition with the Singing Sergeants. That was why he hated the Berlin Wall so much, he figured it had cost him his shot at a run of soft duty at the Sugar Bowl and the Freedom Foundation.

Not that life was so bad at Nellis. He played clarinet in the base orchestra and every Friday and Saturday night he led a three-piece combo at the officers' club and it was a well-known fact that General Curtis LeMay who was out there on an inspection tour said his music was the high point of his trip. So when he got out of the Air Force with his pension, he was still only thirty-nine years of age, a young man really, with many years of experience playing in various Air Force orchestras and combos, though never with the Singing Sergeants. The trouble was that the bottom had fallen out of the music business, the rise of the discotheques with their canned music had put a lot of musicians out of work. Sidemen who had played with the Dorsey brothers and Les Brown and His Band of Renown and Tex Beneke and the Glenn Miller Orchestra. People like these got the few jobs open, he supposed that was only fair, not that he took a back seat to anybody when it came to playing the clarinet, except maybe BG. But the thing about an Air Force pension was that it did not stretch very far and so to tide him over until the discotheque fad ran out he went into the bail-bond field. Most of the bail-bond people in Vegas stayed clear of hookers, they were notoriously unreliable, but Bill Parsons figured that a girl could have a good career in Vegas, the heat wasn't that bad and there weren't that many cities around with hundred-dollar tricks available every night. There was Los Angeles and there was New York, but the protection in both places was so enormous that a girl could make out much better in Vegas. So he decided to specialize and the way he specialized was by advertising "I'll Get You Out of Jail and Onto the Street," and one girl came to him and then another and pretty soon he had a good little business going. To avoid getting burned he made each girl give him a fifty-dollar cashier's check up front to cover the bond for a vag-loitering charge. Think of it as an investment, he would tell them, one call and you're out, you don't have to prove you're solvent, that's already been taken care of. Not many of the girls jumped bail after they got sprung. Vag-loitering wasn't a bad bust and if you were going to peddle your pussy there was less hassle in Vegas than other places. The thing you got to remember about these chicks, Bill Parsons said, is they're lazy and that was the sort of thing that appealed to them.

The upshot was that the advertising gimmick caught on and business got so good that he had more or less forsaken a career in the entertainment area. Not that he didn't see all the shows. Tommy Leonetti, Jerry Vale, Anna Maria Alberghetti, there was one talented chick, a great set of pipes. All dagos, you notice. All the comics are hebes, all the singers dagos and the colored, they got a natural sense of rhythm. That was a line he liked to use, it was a funny bit, a good laugh will get you over any hump in the road. Some of the other people in the bail-bond field were beginning to see that, too. There was one guy whose slogan was "I'll Get You Out If It Takes Ten Years," and a gal who passed out pocket combs with her number on one side and a saying on the other, "Keep The Fuzz Out Of Your Hair." Cute stuff like that. But he was first with "I'll Get You Out of Jail and Onto the Street" and this year he was trying out "Specialist in Bondage" just to see if it increased his business by any appreciable amount.

Bill Parsons said he was a tight writer. That was the secret in this business. The trick was to make sure the client had something going for him, a car, a house, a piece of property. That way he wasn't stuck if the client jumped bail. Insurance covered forfeitures, but a couple of big jumpers would cost you the insurance in no time flat. That was why it was better to pay off the small jumpers than call in the insurance company. Those bastards raised their rates with every claim and if you weren't willing to swallow a few small ones, the premiums would drive you right out of the business. You just couldn't be too careful. One guy got his pastor over at St. Victor's to vouch for him, George just isn't the type of man to stick up an Exxon station, he's a weekly communicant, the priest said, then George splits, sticking him with a five-thousand-dollar bond, and when he calls over at St. Victor's the pastor says, I'll say a novena for you. Another guy puts up a brand-new Ford Galaxie 500 as collateral in a rape case, and

when he checks it out after the guy skips town, he finds
it's a loan car from Reggie Ritt's All Seasons Ford.
Things like that. You cover everything and you're going
to end up like the guy who owes half a million in
forfeitures. Five oh oh comma oh oh oh. And most of
it was misdemeanor shit, the biggest claim was for
B&E.

A good rule of thumb, Bill Parsons said, was to
stay away from junkies, drunks and fags. Junkies and
drunks were a good bet to cut and run and fags he just
did not like to see on the bricks. Better for them and
better for Vegas to let them do a spell in cellblock
eleven. Many of the bondsmen in Vegas didn't like to
deal with the colored, but he had had good luck in that
area. Your ordinary colored has usually done time
before and he knows it's not just bread and water in a
dark cell. Take the deed on his house or the pink on his
Cadillac and he's just as good a risk as anybody. Even
a Murder Two colored. That was one thing about your
Vegas juries. When one colored cuts another colored
over on the West Side, nobody gets too hung up about
it. They call it a "West Side misdemeanor" in the
D.A.'s office. One time he went bail for a colored who
stuck up the NAACP office and his lawyer got him off
by saying, That wasn't a stickup, that was a loan. Another time he went bail for a colored charged with
manslaughter for shooting his way into his house with
a shotgun and killing his wife and putting out the eye
of his mother-in-law. And his lawyer said he didn't
have no key and there was no bell and that was the only
way he could get into the house. Not guilty. There were
stories about the colored he could tell all day. But they
were good risks in a high-risk business and that was a

fact. In the long run that was all that counted.

Bill Parsons said maybe we could take in a show one night, Matt Monro was opening at the Flamingo, a major talent in the singing area, why didn't I bring along Artha. Speaking of whom, he had better call her, make sure she took a shower and was getting a little rest.

You can bail me out any time with service like that, I said.

Yeah, well, she's doing me a little favor, he said.

What the favor was I found out that afternoon. You think he just wanted me to try out the towels? Artha said. Dry my ass on the Springmaids? Take a little nap and watch "Password" on the twenty-seven-inch Magnavox color console with the Quasar controls? He gets the room free, his uncle's got juice at the Union Plaza.

So? I said.

So the D.A.'s office is downtown and the Public Defender's office is downtown and the Union Plaza is downtown.

So?

So the lawyers in the D.A.'s office and the Public Defender's office all have private practices on the side, she said. They only make thirteen-three a year to start and like they need everything they can pick up in their spare time. You know the kind of cases. Spades who knock over liquor stores, cowboys who beat the shit out of their old lady, stuff like that. Everything from possession to Murder One. People who need bail.

I was beginning to get it.

Bill Parsons makes bail, she said. These guys refer a lot of cases to him. It means a lot of business.

So he likes to do favors for them to make sure they keep on referring the eightballs to him. Today his favor was me. He springs for the bail, right? Sets me up in a nice room, right? Within walking distance of the courthouse, right? Well, then he comes up to the room and starts calling around town. You hungry? he says. Room 1499, the Union Plaza. So in three hours I blew two assistant D.A.s and one deputy public defender. It all works out. They get a free piece of ass and I save bail. And the next time some crazy spade boosts a gas station Bill gets the bail. Law and order. Friend of the working girl. I'm just pissed off I missed "Password."

3

I called home. The operator said the line was busy and to place the call again in ten minutes.

I placed the call again in ten minutes. Still busy.

I waited another ten minutes. No answer.

SIXTEEN

Buster Mano liked working the West Side. It was a change of pace. None of your usual surveillance-type investigations. Locatings, mainly, and the service of legal papers. It was a funny thing, but your average West Side citizen seemed to get sued a lot more than your average white person. Buster guessed it was because they liked nice cars and fancy threads. Come to think of it, it wasn't a bad way to live. A small down on an Eldorado brougham and twenty-two years to pay. By the time Maury Riordan Cadillac, Serving Southern Nevada Since 1948, got around to filing legal papers, this jungle bunny had a six-month free ride in a 600 hp short, plus a new $29.95 Earl Scheib lemonade paint job. Buster Mano had to go with a guy like that. He liked style whatever the circumstances. He never had any trouble on the West Side. Some guys went over there carrying a piece and coming on like the head honky. "Don't give me any lip, boy," they'd say, "you owe Maury Riordan down at Riordan Cadillac one thousand nine hundred twenty-three dollars and seventeen cents. Boy." That was a good way

to get sugar in your gas tank. That was what they did
on the West Side. They'd steal a pound of C&H from
the Safeway and pour it into your tank. A good rich
mixture. The kind that ruined your engine. Especially
if you came on like the chief charlie. Not Buster Mano.
"Mr. Jefferson," he would say. Forty thousand spades
on the West Side and thirty-nine thousand had names
like Jefferson or Washington. Like they were all
brought up at Monticello and Mount Vernon and were
just stopping by in Vegas for a private game on their
way to a cotton auction. "Mr. Jefferson, I'm Buster
Mano of the Buster Mano and Associates private investigating agency and I've been asked to deliver these
papers to you." And Associates. What a laugh. What
associates. A thirty-nine-year-old secretary who had
been married to six different blackjack dealers, one each
at Caesar's, the Hacienda, the Thunderbird, the Desert
Inn, the Aladdin and the Frontier, and was now keeping company with a box man at the Mint. "Keeping
company," that was the way she put it, maybe because
that was all she could keep, since she talked all the time
about her dysmenorrhea and her monthlies lasting
twenty-two days, good office talk like that. Not that she
didn't fit in with Mel. Mel was his other associate. Mel
was on suspension from the sheriff's department pend-
ing a department trial. Mel had broken both arms and
a leg on a fag he claimed had stuck up a laundromat in
Boulder. Mel claimed the fag resisted arrest. Only at the
time of the stickup this fag had been dancing nude on
the bar of a gay joint in Los Angeles called the Honey
Pan and there were 113 queens who would swear that
at 11:37 P.M. on the 14th of October last this petunia
was doing the limbo on the bar. With a hard-on. It

turned out Mel didn't like fags. So much for his associates.

Anyway, Buster Mano would tell Mr. Jefferson what the papers were for and how he could file an answer to defend himself. There's no doubt in my mind that you mailed in the checks, Mr. Jefferson, no doubt at all. Everyone knows the Post Office department is a scandal. Not making deliveries. Stealing checks to the Maury Riordan Cadillac agency. It's common knowledge. You got a good case there, Mr. Jefferson. And you know something, that's a pretty TV set you've got there. The ninety-six-inch family entertainment-center model, isn't it? It's like watching the fights on closed circuit at the Convention Center. You found it in an alley? You are one lucky man. Forty-eight years I been walking through alleys and I never found a TV set. Yeah, well, I guess I just wasn't born lucky.

Another reason Buster Mano liked the West Side was that people didn't move around so much there. On the Strip it was different. Buster Mano bet that eighty percent of the people living back of the Strip hadn't been there ninety days. Your average West Sider might move around, but usually only a couple of blocks. Which made locatings easy. Say someone wanted to locate a Mr. Washington. Say a loan company in Dallas. Mr. Chester A. Washington. The trick was to say you were looking for a Mr. Leroy Washington. First you knocked on the door. "Sir, I'm looking for Mr. Leroy K. Washington."

"Well, I'm Chester A. Washington."

"That's the wrong one, sir. This Mr. Washington drives a '56 Edsel."

"I got a '71 Pontiac Le Mans. Radio, heater,

power brakes, power steering, stereo tape deck, tinted windows and movable steering column."

"No, sir, this Mr. Washington was a butcher."

"I'm in sales."

"The Mr. Washington I'm looking for is from Dallas."

"Galveston."

"Too bad. There's an estate just been settled in Dallas and my Mr. Washington has an inheritance coming to him."

"There's a branch of my family in Dallas."

I've got a case, you might like it, Buster Mano said. We were in the drugstore at the Sands and he bought a bottle of Maalox, a bottle of Kaopectate, a bottle of Pepto-Bismol and a jar of Alophen. He laid an Alophen tablet on his tongue right there at the counter and chased it with a swig of Pepto-Bismol. It left a pink circle around his mouth. *Semper paratus,* he said.

What kind of case? I was tired of cases and tired of being a pimp and tired of the network of deceptions that seemed to characterize my stay in Vegas, but there was no imperative to go home. Yet.

This broad called me long distance from Savannah, Georgia, Buster Mano said. Her husband, Ralph Neary, was flying into Vegas that day on an Oasis junket. The last of the big spenders, she had called him. Mr. Big Deal. Ralph Neary's wife suspected that Ralph Neary was going to be met there. She did not want to name names, but she bet she knew who that hussy was. She was nothing but a legal secretary from Atlanta. If that was the one, not that Mrs. Ralph Neary wanted to cast aspersions. She wasn't that sort, like some she could name. She just wanted to check up. She just wanted to know what Ralph Neary was doing all the time he was supposed to be gambling. Buster Mano asked what Ralph Neary looked like. A physical description, so to speak. He's got hair on his back, Ralph Neary's wife said. And he's got a hernia. That's a good description, Buster Mano said, that's going to be a real help. There was just one other thing he wanted to know. How had Mrs. Ralph Neary happened to pick him? Well, she said, she had gone to the public library in Savannah, they have a collection of telephone books there from all the major cities, Tampa, Biloxi, places like that, and she had found his name in the Vegas Yellow Pages. She just liked the name, her sister, you see, had a dog once, part cocker spaniel and part beagle, and she called that dog Buster and she just loved that dog, and so when Mrs. Ralph Neary saw his name, she just said to herself, I'm going to play me a hunch.

And you wonder why I can't take a shit, Buster Mano said.

After that it was easy. The first thing was to find out what Ralph Neary looked like. Because there weren't many guys in Vegas with hair on their back, because there weren't that many with hernias. I mean, some hotels don't let in Jews, here in Vegas, it's different, you got a hernia, you got hair on your back, no room at the inn. Jesus, Buster Mano said, Jesus, if I had a truss business I'd be a millionaire. He's got a hernia, can you beat that? He called the Oasis. Ralph Neary, please.

"Hello."

"This is room service, sir, checking your breakfast order tomorrow morning. Eight-thirty sharp, right? Six V-8 juice, six breakfast steaks, scrambled eggs on the side, toast, jams, jellies and hot coffee, right?"

"Wrong."

"This is not the party in 1411?"

"No."

"I beg your pardon then, sir. To what party am I then speaking?"

"2612."

"Would you care to leave a breakfast order, then, sir?"

A guy's in Vegas on a junket, so you figure he's not going to spend a lot of time in 2612, right? That is, until the legal secretary from Atlanta shows up. Up to the corridor outside 2612 and within fifteen minutes Ralph Neary walks out the door. There was no sign of a hernia that Buster Mano could make out. Ralph Neary walked good. As a matter of fact Buster Mano would say that Ralph Neary had a very nice walk. He also had a black hairpiece and wore goggle glasses like he was a Flying Fortress pilot in WW II. Five feet nine and two hundred two pounds, hard as nails and proud of it, Buster Mano knew the type. Catches all the big events, the Derby, Superbowl, Indianapolis Five. They all had hair on their backs.

1400—1430: Subject played come line, crap pits, Oasis Hotel. 1430—1500: Subject played don't pass line, crap pits, Oasis Hotel. 1505: Subject ordered Cutty and water from cocktail waitress, crap pits, Oasis Hotel. 1507: Subject tips waitress with five-dollar bill, stuffing said bill between her pectorals. 1510: Subject's point is ten, crap pits, Oasis Hotel. 1512: Subject craps out, crap pits, Oasis Hotel.

The chick showed up that night. She looked like

Frances Langford, right out of the big-band era, a lot of blond hair piled on top of her head, big wedgies, thirty-five years old on a good day. She looked like she had spent a lifetime meeting guys in Vegas or Miami Beach or Louisville for the Derby. But there were lines around the eyes now and there weren't going to be many more post times at Churchill Downs. Buster Mano liked her on sight and didn't really want to bug her room and listen to her fuck Ralph Neary. That was something he had discovered about himself. No matter how nice the broad was, it was a turn-off for him to tune in on her balling someone. It was just one of those things.

Putting the bug in was a cinch. 2614 was empty and so he went to the desk and said listen, last time I was in I stayed in 2614, it's my lucky room, I made over eleven hundred dollars in that room, I wonder if it's free because I really feel lucky and I got the bankroll to prove it. Twenty minutes later Buster Mano had the room right next door to Ralph Neary and the blonde, and the manager had sent him up a fresh pineapple with his card and then later on a bottle of White Label with ice and setups. The word about the bankroll apparently traveled fast. The bug fit right into a wall socket and the only tricky part was to get Ralph Neary out of 2612 long enough to plug it in. So he just waited around until Ralph Neary and the blonde went out to dinner and when they did he called the housekeeper and asked her to clean up 2612, the towels were dirty and the room needed to be tidied up, there was a five in it for her if she got it done fast. Buster Mano never knew a spade to show up so quick. Eight o'clock at night and this spade had the vacuum cleaner moving all over 2612.

Then Buster Mano pops in from next door and says, listen, I'm in 2614, my wife's got ptomaine, it was something she ate in your coffee shop downstairs and there's no toilet paper, we need a couple of rolls of TP really bad, double-ply, if you got it, could you run down to the utility room, the toilet's a mess, we don't want to sue the Oasis, you know, for serving a tainted hamburger, and the spade leaves 2612 empty for a couple of minutes and Buster fits the bug into the socket right next to the bed. And on top of that he's got enough toilet paper to swab every ass in Vegas.

Oh, Ralph, the blonde says during the night, I never knew it could be so good.

And then: Of course I don't mind taking it in the ass, darling, I want to do anything that makes you happy.

And finally: Ralph, baby, we going to go to the Cotton Bowl this year?

Buster Mano said, Don't bet on it, baby.

In the morning Ralph Neary went down to play a little blackjack before breakfast, he liked the action, *mano a mano,* just him and the dealer this early in the day. Buster Mano waited until he got downstairs and then called 2612. He still did not have the blonde's name and all Ralph Neary had called her in the bug's hearing while he was grunting on top of her was, you cunt, you bitch and occasionally you twat. Buster Mano did not think that was going to be good enough for Ralph Neary's wife, she would want a name to stick to that twat, so he dialed 2612 and when the blonde answered, he sang,

> *"Happy birthday to you,*
> *Happy birthday to you,*

Happy birthday, dear Myrna,
Happy birthday to you. "

And then Buster Mano said, "And that's signed,
'Ed and Paula and all the gang at the office.' "

"Oh, that's so funny," the blonde said.

"We'll send you a copy," Buster Mano said.

"But I'm not Myrna."

"You're not Myrna Kissel, Room 2612, Oasis
Hotel, Las Vegas, Nevada."

"It's room 2612, but I'm not Myrna Kissel."

She's not going to bite, Buster Mano thought.
"Who are you, then?"

"Roberta Boykin."

"Listen, Roberta, I'm really sorry, I'll ring the
operator. And the happiest of birthdays when you have
one."

He had the tape and the name and all he needed
now was the picture. The hotels did not allow cameras
in the casinos and you just didn't go up to Ralph Neary
and Roberta Boykin at the swimming pool and say,
Listen, Ralph, your old lady back in Savannah would
like a little candid of you and Roberta, you know, to use
in the divorce. So he called the public relations man at
the Oasis and said he was from *Sunset* magazine and
Sunset was going to do a "Holiday in Las Vegas" special issue and he would just love to take some shots of
the swimming pool and shuffleboard areas to show people that there was more to Las Vegas than just gambling, it was a family resort, too, with Olympic-size
swimming pools and shuffleboard and tennis instructions from the top professional teachers in the game,
and gambling was only part, one part, of the good-time-

type thing. The public relations man thought that was really a terrific idea, a really different approach, and that when the *Sunset* photographer came he could expect every consideration from the Oasis. Which Buster Mano was shown. He got shots of the shuffleboard and the tennis instruction and the high diving board and twenty-two exposures of Roberta Boykin greasing Ralph Neary's chest, lighting his cigar, kissing his cheek, tracing his appendicitis scar, all clear as a bell from a Nikon with a 600 mm lens set up on a tripod on the lanai side of the Olympic-sized swimming pool. Terrific stuff. So terrific that Buster Mano sent the rest of it to *Sunset* and to *U.S. Camera*. Just in case they had a "What An Amateur Can Do With A Nikon" section. You never can tell, Buster Mano said.

2

The weekly telephone call. Area Code 702 to Area Code 213, station call collect. I had taken to calling collect. It was the first indication I had given that I was thinking of coming home. Only that, nothing more. I knew that she would pick it up. We communicated in nuance like that, like a couple of weary demonologists alert to the weight of every syllable in the official communiqué.

News clippings from the accidental death page first. I had found that I could entertain her with my theory that every newspaper had a freak-death desk, and on a light day when gold was holding steady and the economy was sound and housing starts were up and no F-111s had been shot down and everyone in the majors had split a doubleheader and there had been no major assassinations outside Central America, the freak-death editor could make up an inside page. It was really just a way of making a connection when otherwise we were not saying much to each other, like technical discussions between second-echelon diplomats when truce talks get bogged down. It was a good week for freak deaths. A man in a Superman suit had frozen to death in the refrigerator of his Hollywood apartment. An eighty-year-old woman and her sixty-two-year-old daughter had strangled the eighty-three-year-old husband of one and father of the other with a pair of black nylon panty hose purchased at Frederick's of Hollywood. It was a record year for homicides in Clark County: twenty-three gunshot cases, five stabbings, two beatings, two strangulations and one criminal abortion. There were other items celebrating life. The "phobia-phobes" were picketing the district health office, protesting that psychiatry "comes from Russia, from Pavlov, and is a plot to undermine Western civilization." An amnesiac woman had checked herself into a hotel downtown called the Sal Sagev (Las Vegas spelled backward) under the name of "Eno Onmai," which turned out to be "I am no one" spelled backward.

"Not bad stuff," I said.

"When are you coming home?" she said.

It looked like the technical discussions were also going to get bogged down. "As soon as I get my life in order."

"Why not try living it?" she said. "For a change."

"Oh, it's that kind of day, is it?"

It was the old argument. She claimed that I

vandalized other people's lives instead of coming to grips with my own. It was an argument without a rebuttal, which is what made it particularly infuriating. I knew why I was in Vegas. I just did not like having it spelled out. There were times when I think we fought only because we were good at it. Betrayal never worked for us. We each had too highly developed a sense of guilt, a sense that nothing was free, that every action carried a price tag. So we fought. I won the battles, but she seemed to be winning the war. Hers was a war of attrition, of nuance and inflection and pregnant pauses, the Viet Cong against the tactical nukes. It was an uneven struggle.

I tried to regain the initiative. "Anything happen with you?"

She said that a gossip columnist had called her earlier that evening and asked if she spoke Spanish. She said yes and the gossip columnist had asked her if she would then speak to her gardener and tell him to turn off the rainbirds.

I asked what she had said to the gossip columnist's gardener.

"*No más agua.*"

Subject exhausted.

"Maybe I'll call you later."

"Maybe I'll be awake."

I did not call her later. I did not want to find out if maybe she was awake. I turned on "The Dick Cavett Show." Another fantasy. Another life to live. Another incarnation. A forty-four-year-old crusading Congressman this time. Still in my thirties, I was uncomfortable at being forty-four, but I needed the heft of age to make the fantasy work, and forty-four seemed a good age, old, but not too old. A veteran of Okinawa, called back into the Marines during Korea as a twenty-three-year-old reserve lieutenant, winner of the Navy Cross at the Choisin Reservoir. Presently, despite my military background, the most outspoken dove in the Congress, party affiliation unspecified.

I was grooving with it now. The other guest was John Wayne and while I was backstage in the green room I watched the Duke on the monitor lambasting all doves as un-American comsymp traitors, aiding and abetting Hanoi, Peking, Moscow and all slave states east and west. Now it was my turn. The cool Marine. Speaker at teach-ins. Escort of Gloria Steinem.

"How old are you, Mr. Wayne?" The question was pleasant, magna cum laude Harvard Law School pleasant.

"Sixty-four," the Duke answered.

An uneasy look crossed Cavett's face, as if he was wondering what I was up to, fearing that Wayne was about to be dry-gulched in a box canyon.

The camera was on my face. "Hmmmm, twenty years older than I am." Pause for effect. "I was fourteen when the war started." A quick smile. "Remember the summer of forty-one? Not that I'm plugging a picture, Dick, like Mr. Wayne here."

An appreciative Yale chuckle from Cavett. USC alumnus Wayne glowers.

"I was seventeen when I enlisted in the Marines three years later," I say. "Eighteen when I got my butt shot off—that won't get bleeped out, will it, Dick; I'd hate to get you in trouble with the network censors—at Okinawa. As a buck-ass private in the Third Marine

Division. 'Howling Mad' Smith's outfit. Old H.M. Smith, I guess with 'Chesty' Puller the best general officer the Marine Corps ever had."

Someone in the audience claps. I am deep into my role now.

"I was called back during Korea. Got my butt shot off again at Choisin." I am careful not to mention my Navy Cross, nor my commission.

Cavett chews on a finger. He is beginning to see the shape of the game. That Yale education. Not much on the gridiron, Yale, but a two-touchdown favorite over USC in the intellect department.

"So you see, Mr. Wayne . . ." I pause and light a cigarette; the Congressman is up to two packages of Pall Malls a day; ex-Marines don't smoke those sissy filter cigarettes. ". . . I don't much like being called a traitor by a flying leatherneck who got no closer to the action than the sands of Iwo Jima."

A master stroke. *Flying Leathernecks* and *The Sands of Iwo Jima* were two of the Duke's biggest hits.

The biggest box-office attraction of 1949 begins to unwind from his chair. I can see the sweat mottling the make-up on the net of his toupee.

"I take it you were thirty-four when the war started. About the same age as Gable and Jimmy Stewart." It's getting rough now. "Captain Clark Gable and Brigadier General Jimmy Stewart, Eighth Air Force."

"Now, wait just a minute." The familiar twang that has launched a hundred cavalry charges. Tall in the saddle at the bend of the river where the cottonwoods grow.

"No, I don't like being called a coward by someone old enough to enlist in '41. When I was only fourteen."

The Duke is standing now, towering over Cavett, fist cocked.

I keep my seat, my voice still quiet. "There's no stunt man here, Mr. Wayne. No director to say 'cut.' No Jack Ford to help you out." Now the element of menace. Judo champion, USMC Recruit Depot, Camp Pendleton, California. "You make one move and I'll . . ."

Cavett is desperately searching behind his chair for a box of Gaines Burgers. He holds it up. "And now a word from all the wonderful people at Gaines."

I am bathed in sweat. The effort of fantasy. Euphoria. I feel sated, ready for sleep, the crusading Congressman, ready now for a tough Senate race, eight years in the Upper House and then, "Mr. Chairman, Illinois casts all one hundred and sixty-nine votes for the next President of the United States . . ."

A vandal.

SEVENTEEN

The funny thing was it happened at match point. It also happened when it was 114° courtside, which could have been a contributing factor. But then if you're going to tap out with a myocardial infarction there are worse places to have it than Vegas. And he looked terrific, Hugh Hill. Inside he always wore those forty-pound cordovans and dressed up from there, a lot of gray flannel and patch pockets and single-vent stuff, but on the courts it was a different story. All sky-blue. Everyone else is decked out in white like a nun in the Congo, but not Hugh Hill. A custom-made sky-blue terrycloth outfit. With white trim. Like the white "H.H." on the pocket of the tennis shirt. And the white stripes on the blue shoes. And it didn't stop there. He had yellow tennis balls. And an aluminum racket. Pancho Gonzales had sold him on it, he said. You needed something lightweight in a hot climate, Pancho had said. Hugh Hill talked tennis even better than he talked frosty cream. Or marketing Brother JayJay. He used all the right names. Rod and Lew and Pancho and Pancho II. He liked to call Segura Pancho II because that made everyone sure to ask who Pancho II was. Hugh Hill was like that.

And so here's Rog Paradise down one set and five games to two in the second, match point, score forty-love, waiting for this guy in blue terrycloth to serve a yellow ball with an aluminum racket. Rog Paradise was Hugh Hill's ad guy. That's how Rog Paradise described himself. An ad guy. The Peter Partridge Peanut Butter guy. The Bank of Savings guy. Actually he called it the BOS guy. The frosty-cream guy. And now he was going to be the Brother JayJay guy. He had done some show business, Rog Paradise. Revues, sketches, night-club routines. Wrote the skits, the music, the lyrics. Good stuff, ahead of its time. Tommy Smothers loved it. Woody Allen, David Steinberg, that type people. He wrote a couple of BOS jingles free-lance and then he became a full-time ad guy and finally a creative director. Not that he had given up on show business. He was working on a musical. Tommy Smothers would love it. The agency was just an interim type thing. It paid for the house in Hancock Park. It's where the old Angelenos live, Rog Paradise said. And the really high-type creative directors. Big houses, not too expensive, and the schools were still good. Which meant that the spades hadn't moved in yet. They were moving west like a goddam flood which was why these big sixteen-room houses in Hancock Park were going for sixty-seven five, easy financing. Which was also why the old Angelenos were moving out and selling their places to high-type creative directors who drank martinis and said slow on the vermouth.

Anyway Hugh Hill threw up the yellow ball and then he never hit it with his aluminum racket. He just

said, I don't feel good, and he came over and sat down
and the sweat had begun to leak through the blue terrycloth. Then he said, Maybe I better lie down, and Rog
Paradise and Jackie Kasey helped him into the health
club and he stretched out on a rubbing table. Lew Foxx
said he could probably use some steam, but then Lew
Foxx thought that if you had leprosy you could use
some steam, and maybe a pair of rosary beads stuffed
up your ass before you came. Hugh Hill said no, he
didn't want any steam or a sauna or a French douche
or a whirlpool or a rubdown, just a doctor. As it happened, there was an M.D. from Phoenix getting a massage in the next booth and he came in with a towel
around his privates and he said it looked like a coronary
occlusion and he would phone an ambulance. He
wasn't licensed to practice in Vegas but he would stay
with Hugh Hill until the ambulance came and then he
would finish his massage. Lew Foxx said, That's a nice
thing for you to do. And then he said that the rubdown
would be on the house. Lew Foxx hoped that the ambulance would get there in a hurry, because if there was
one thing he didn't want it was a stiff in his health club,
it was bad for business. All these fat guys with pink skin
from the steam, they would see a stiff and figure it was
the sauna and they might get dressed and never come
back because with most guys, if there is one place they
don't want to check out it's in a steam room. At least
that was what Lew Foxx figured. Not that he had to
worry. The ambulance got there in no time flat and
Hugh Hill was rolled out to it in a wheelchair instead
of a stretcher, which made it look a lot better. Maybe
like he twisted his knee playing tennis in his blue outfit
instead of having a heart seizure. You got to think of

the image, Lew Foxx said. Like even if this guy had cooled on the rubbing table he would have recommended that the ambulance boys bring him out in the wheelchair instead of the stretcher. It just made more sense. A guy with a sheet over his head coming out of the health club. Jesus.

Jackie Kasey thought it all worked out for the best. Not that he was happy that Hugh Hill had a heart attack. That would be the wrong interpretation to put on it, the wrong one entirely. Jackie Kasey went to see Hugh Hill every day he was in the intensive-care unit at Southern Nevada Memorial, ten days in all, in the early evening when he usually took a nap before his first show. Missing the nap, that didn't matter, he would tell Hugh Hill, the important thing is you getting better. He had to admit, though, that he was glad to see Hugh Hill take the ambulance back to L.A. Three weeks' recuperation in the condominium in Playa del Rey with round-the-clock nurses, then back to his desk peddling frosty cream, that was the schedule he had worked out. Nothing at all about Brother JayJay, about making him a product. No Rog Paradise to hype the act. The coronary gave everyone an out and that was why Jackie Kasey thought it had all worked out for the best.

To begin with, Jackie Kasey had not been expecting Rog Paradise. Hugh Hill said he was going to bring up a writer and there were a lot of writers available, guys who had worked "The Dean Martin Show" and "The Carol Burnett Show," guys who were on the unemployment line now because the webs were off variety shows this year, guys who knew *schtick*. He wasn't expecting the Peter Partridge Peanut Butter guy. What do you think of Lenny Bruce, Rog Paradise had said, what do you think of Dick Gregory? I think one's dead and the other's a *schwartze,* Jackie Kasey wanted to say, and a *schwartze* fasting himself down to seventy-eight pounds might be a lot of laughs at Vassar College, but it won't work in a lounge. The reason he didn't say it was because he was already feeling bad enough without starting an argument. It was all because of Celebrity Cancer Night. Hugh Hill and Rog Paradise had arrived in town early and Jackie Kasey took them over to the Flamingo where all the stars on the Strip were doing a free gig for the Cancer Society. "A Buck & A Button For Cancer" was the slogan. Totie Fields will be there, Jackie Kasey had said, Tom Jones, Frank Gorshin, all the superstars. Terrific, Hugh Hill had said. But when they got to the Flamingo the only superstar who had shown up was Tanya, the elephant from Circus Circus. Cute as hell, but still an elephant. Tom Jones had a cold, the M.C. said, and Frank Gorshin had to go to L.A. on business and Totie Fields had got the date wrong, she was doing another benefit, you understand how it is, Jackie. There were a lot of kids in the audience and they were throwing peanuts at Tanya and Jackie Kasey felt as useless as a singer in a tit show.

"Maybe I ought to wait until Tanya goes off," Jackie Kasey said to the M.C. His name was Dave Baum and he was a local disk jockey.

"The kids love her, Jackie," the M.C. said. "It'll be a funny bit, you and Tanya."

"I don't know," Jackie Kasey said.

The disk jockey was already heading for the microphone. "Laze and gemmen, my very warm personal friend, Jackie Kasey," Dave said. "He starred with Elvis, he traveled with Elvis and now he's a star in his own right, let's hear it for Jackie Kasey, a really big hand."

Jackie Kasey bounced up on stage, throwing a kiss to the M.C. "Dave, I love you," he said. And then to the audience, "I just love that guy."

He began to adjust the microphone and as he did a child hit him in the chest with a peanut aimed at Tanya. Jackie Kasey picked up the peanut, cracked it open and ate it. He pointed his finger at the girl. "What's your name?"

"Barbara."

"BARBARA! Well, you are the cutest little BAR-BARA I have ever seen."

Another peanut bounced on the stage.

Jackie Kasey looked desperate. "Laze and gemmen, here's a little song for you, one of the all-time favorites, 'Bye, Bye, Blackbird,' laze and gemmen."

He began moving around the stage, trying to keep a constant distance between himself and Tanya, snapping his fingers and then the microphone cord, working into an impromptu dance step whenever Tanya's trunk sought him out, fluid, always on the move and when he forgot the lyrics shifting into "Boom, boom, boom, Da, da, da, Dee, dee, dee, Bye, bye, blackbird." A final flourish, a pat on the head for Tanya, a two-handed kiss to the audience and, "God love you, laze and gemmen, God love you, peace and love."

Dave, the M.C., was onstage clapping. "Let's hear it for Jackie Kasey, laze and gemmen, a great guy, a great talent, a friend of the Cancer Society and you can hear him nightly at the Tropicana Lounge."

Jackie Kasey looked mortified. "The Taj Mahal Theater, Dave."

"Right," Dave said. "a star in his own right at the Taj Mahal Theater."

Hugh Hill was not impressed. Hugh Hill said he wanted to market Brother JayJay and not "Bye, Bye, Blackbird." There wasn't much of a product in "Bye, Bye, Blackbird," why didn't he do Brother JayJay, that was what he was known for now. Because I was being upstaged by a fucking elephant, Jackie Kasey said. And then Rog Paradise asked what Jackie thought of Lenny Bruce and Dick Gregory. Maybe the *schwartze* could work with Tanya, Jackie Kasey said, they both come out of the same goddam jungle.

Rog Paradise said that you sold a comic like any other product.

Hugh Hill said, Absolutely.

Jackie Kasey's first show that night was terrible and the second was worse. He complained of a cold. He complained about the house. He always has an excuse, Hugh Hill said. He'll always cop out. His life is chaos. Four shrinks and a fortune teller in Camden, New Jersey. He thinks I'm going to wave a magic wand, Hugh Hill said. Wentworth told him he was going to meet a man on a plane. The mysterious stranger. I must be the only guy in the frosty-cream business who's also a mysterious stranger.

Hugh Hill told Jackie Kasey that there would be no more cocking around. Hugh Hill also said that from now on he was going to be a dictator. A benevolent dictator, but he was calling the shots. And the first shot was aimed at me. What the hell are you sniffing around Jackie for? Hugh Hill said. I had you checked out. I know how to use a library. I can look you up in *The Reader's Guide.* I can read what you've written. The

second-rate comic who's never going to make it. I bet
that's what you're interested in. I bet that's your angle.

No, it's not, Jackie Kasey said.

How do I know that? Hugh Hill said.

You don't, I said.

Jackie Kasey's eyes swiveled toward me. I was
going to get you laid, he would be thinking, I got you
a date with Teddi, it's not my fault you didn't make it
with her. You're like the ad guy, you're like the frosty-
cream guy.

Or perhaps he was not thinking that at all. Perhaps I had no idea what he was thinking. We weren't
really friends, I wasn't even sure I liked him. We were
like two people thrown together in a lifeboat after a
mid-ocean disaster. Grab an oar, catch the prevailing
current, the only way we can survive is to pull together.
How much do two people in a lifeboat have in common?

Hugh Hill broke the impasse. Rehearsal tomorrow morning ten A.M., Hugh Hill said. Time was
money, Hugh Hill also said, and he did not have the
time to invest in Brother JayJay if it was not going to
pay off. Quick.

Rog Paradise rounded up a piano. It was out of
tune, but Rog Paradise said it did not matter, this was
only a rehearsal. Rog Paradise had written a new intro.
We'll work on it until we all feel comfortable, Hugh
Hill said. Jackie Kasey said he felt like shit. His throat
hurt, his chest hurt and he was depressed. Rog Paradise
said, A-one, a-two, a-three:

"You shouldn't be no sinner
Unless you are a winner
At the game of...
Hide-and-love. Oh yeah."

Jackie Kasey shook his head. Bank of Savings
would love it. Peter Partridge Peanut Butter would lap
it up. A-one, a-two, a-three, Rog Paradise said.

"Cheatin' on your wife's a sin
If your wife knows where you
    been
An' let me tell you true
Getting caught's bad too
By the gentleman who's livin'
With the lady you been givin'
That lov—ing to. Oh yeah."

Jackie Kasey said, Terrific. Rog Paradise said
that when the rhythm went right the payoffs would be
better. A-one, a-two, a-three:

"When you're checking into
    that motel
Or that hotel
By the sea . . .
Do not make it a game of
    show-tell
If she's your neighbor's
Sweet Marie. Oh yeah."

It's all in the *oh yeahs*, Hugh Hill said.

Oh yeah, Jackie Kasey said.

Stop cocking around, Hugh Hill said.

I got to feel it, Jackie Kasey said.

You're not trying, Hugh Hill said.

A-one, a-two, a-three, Rog Paradise said.

Ten o'clock, eleven o'clock, noontime. Hugh Hill said it was getting comfortable. Hugh Hill said when it was really comfortable Jackie could try it out on the Jerry Fisher Show.

I don't do bits on local TV, Jackie Kasey said.

It's got an ARB of only 54,000, Hugh Hill said. Who's going to hear it? It's not like you're throwing it away on national TV.

I don't do bits on local TV, Jackie Kasey repeated.

Well, what do you do on local TV? Hugh Hill said.

I talk about myself, Jackie Kasey said. My career. About how I'm going to be packaged. About how I'm trying to be a better comedian and a better human being. About how I think that's one of the most important things in the world.

I'm going to play some tennis, Hugh Hill said.

EIGHTEEN

I spent about a month in Vegas after Hugh Hill got his heart attack. Jackie finished his engagement at the hotel and then he got a movie. It was typecasting, he said. He was going to play a Vegas comic. A small part, two lines. "Who's the chick?" was the first line, and "Honey, how are you?" was the second, but it was a shot, a new career, and he was going to make the most of it, he saw his shot and he was going to take it. They wanted to know if I had my own tuxedo, he said, and I said, does a bear shit in the woods, I got eleven tuxedos, I got a deal with a guy who makes tuxedos in L.A., he makes tuxedos for Tony Martin and Jerry Vale and Frank Gorshin, guys like that, superstars, do I have my own tuxedo, oh, boy, can you beat that.

I saw Artha occasionally and Buster, and I told them both that I would arrange a dinner so that they could meet, but I never got around to it. Mainly I just watched a lot of TV. And then one day I got a call from Artha. Her mother was in town and she asked me to dinner. It would be easier, she said, you can answer the phone, you know what I mean? Her mother's name was

Dot and Dot was forty-seven. Dot was going through the menopause and she said that the menopause was her license to swing, if you get what I mean. Dot bought Artha a Polaroid camera and a bear rug and Dot said she and Artha looked like sisters, maybe they could swing together. I asked Artha if Dot knew what she did and Artha said, listen, I'm free, white and twenty-one, she better not ask. Dot was swinging with a bartender on the graveyard shift at the Frontier and the bartender had once run Artha and Artha thought it was cute, the bartender thought it was cute, too, he would never tell Dot, if you get what I mean. The telephone rang six times during the evening and the calls were all the same.

"Artha there?"

"No."

"Tell her Howard Smiley called."

"Okay."

"From Seattle."

"Okay."

"Tell her I'm in on a junket."

"Okay."

"Ready to howl."

"Okay."

"She'll remember me."

"Sure, Howard."

Dot never asked who called. When I left Artha's apartment that night I remember that the clock on the Sahara gave the time as 1:14 and the temperature was 98. When I got to my apartment the time was 1:33 and the temperature still 98. For the first time the clock on the Sahara did not remind me of death. I recall turning off the air conditioner and opening the windows and sleeping fourteen hours bathed in sweat, as if after fever.

2

It has been two years now since I last was in Vegas and the things I remember about it have nothing to do with why I went, and less with why I left. I remember Jackie, of course, and Buster, Buster who the last two Christmases has sent me a calendar featuring the nude dancers of the Lido de Paris line over the logo "Buster Mano & Associates, Private Investigations." And then a few months ago I ran into Jackie on Sunset Boulevard. He had been cut out of the picture, he said, he was really terrific in his part, the director said so and the director said he wanted to work with him again he was such a terrific actor, a lead next time, but the picture was long and something had to go, sometimes you had to cut the best stuff, that was the way it was in movies.

Let's get together, I said. Sure, he said. And the funny thing was, we did.

It was at an apartment high in the Hollywood Hills, above the smog line, and from the terrace that hot February day we could see the haze hanging over the city like a soiled brown magic carpet. The apartment belonged to a girl friend, Jackie Kasey said. An ex-girl friend. They were still pals. She gave him the key to the apartment when she was out of town. Don't tell Roxy I got the key, Jackie Kasey said. Tell her we went to a restaurant. It was just another minor conspiracy. The girl friend had arrived back from Europe that morning, dumped her clothes and gone out to catch some sun in Jerry Hennessy's catamaran. I didn't ask who Jerry Hennessy was. The floor was littered with stained nylon panties, cans of strawberry-scented vaginal spray and boxes of super tampons. It reminds me of Vegas, I said.

What? he said.

I didn't push it. We were a little uncomfortable with each other. The tenuous connection we had established in Vegas was broken. In that prison of yesterdays we could maintain the illusion that we were close, but with the Vegas tension gone I began to wonder if he was even a good character.

From a strictly personal point of view, it probably all worked out for the best, Jackie Kasey said. He said he had dropped the Brother JayJay routine. Brother JayJay had been taking over Jackie Kasey and there were too many other facets to Jackie Kasey. A man can't be a product, he said. A man's got to be true to himself. Twenty years he had been knocking his brains out in this business trying to be funny. Every night. That's not the answer. The answer is to be a person and try to find out who you are and what you are. Isn't that the answer?

I allowed that it seemed to be.

It took Hugh Hill's heart attack to teach him that, Jackie Kasey said. It all worked out for the best. He's got his frosty-cream company and I've got my facets.

3

I am less sure than Jackie Kasey of what I have. I can only say that it was a bad season and then it was over. I had arrived in Vegas an emotional paraplegic, obsessed by death, and there I found a kind of peace. There in that Genet vision of hell my own version seemed tolerable; there among the Snopeses of the free-enterprise system life did not seem so bad. I would like to believe that I had a certain empathy for those whose lives I vandalized. People like Buster and Artha and Jackie allowed me in that troubled time to shuck off commitment to those close to me, to avoid all psychic responsibility while trying to work things out. What you have read is a myelogram of six months of my life. I can offer no guarantee that everything you read actually happened, only that insofar as it was perceived by my fractured sensors it was true. Then the pieces were back together, and in the fall I went home.